GAYLORD MG

Painted Country Woodcrafts

Over 50 Decorative Projects for the Home

by Marina Alexee Grant

Meredith® Press
New York

Acknowledgments

I would like to thank the following people for their assistance and support in the preparation of this project. This book could not have been completed without the individual efforts and combined talents of each one of them:

Patricia Van Note, who conceived the idea, developed the concept, and inspired me to try my hand at authoring a book; George Mordew, Bill Zharndt, and Chris Grant, the craftsmen at the Wooden Hen shop who translated my fuzzy sketches into the wonderful wood pieces in this book; Debra Winter Ramsayer, who basecoated, produced painstaking line art, and brought in the best soups for lunch breaks; Darlene Cutchall, who dropped everything to carefully wrap and ship each of the pieces for photography; The Editors, Maryanne Bannon, Carol Spier, and Ruth Weadock, for their much-needed encouragement of the work-in-progress; Josh Grant who filled in for me at my "day job," and did it so well that he allowed me the freedom to "sing." Special thanks to Brian, friend and partner, who spent hours at the computer making a manuscript out of my verbiage, and who gave all to keep the home and work fires burning brightly—and for becoming quite the gourmet chef. Thank you, all: This is truly the product of a group effort. Very special thanks to my parents, Ann and Jim Alexee.

Meredith® Press is an imprint of Meredith® Books
President, Book Group: Joseph J. Ward
Vice-President, Editorial Director: Elizabeth P. Rice

For Meredith Press:
Executive Editor: Maryanne Bannon
Senior Editor: Carol Spier
Associate Editor: Ruth Weadock
Assistant: Ruth Rojas
Copyeditor: Barbara Tchabovsky
Production Manager: Bill Rose
Design: Diane Wagner
Photography: Robert Gatullo
Special thanks to Carla Vel
for the loan of her apartment
for photography.

ISBN: 0-696-04667-9 (hardcover)
ISBN: 0-696-20425-8 (softcover)

Library of Congress Card Catalog Number: 93-077578
Published by Meredith® Press
Distributed by Meredith Corporation, Des Moines, Iowa

10 9 8 7 6 5 4

Dedication

 za za za za za za za za za za

To my family and friends, Brian, Chris, Josh, Pat, and Daisy.

za za

Dear Crafter,

From start to finish, it has been a pleasure to bring this book to you. From the lovely and charming designs, full-color photography and attractive layout, to all the production steps in between, we have done our best to bring you the most wonderful painted country projects, and to present them in an appealing and uncomplicated manner.

We hope you will find all of the Basics sections helpful, the step-by-step directions easy-to-follow, and the photographs that accompany each piece to be not only a visual reference but also an inspiration to create your own hand-painted family heirlooms.

Perhaps most of all, we hope to convey the extra "special" quality of these pieces, the quality of love and care that is shared by everything hand-made and hand-crafted. It is this quality that we found to be common to each of these folk art treasures, and that we hope will inspire you to make them. Whether you decide to give them as gifts or display them in your home, we hope you find this to be true as you create your own works of art.

Sincerely,

Carol Spier

Carol Spier, Senior Editor

A word about the projects in this book for children's accessories: Use discretion when presenting painted objects (such as the Noah's Ark Set) to young children—particularly babies and toddlers, for whom these projects are not suitable toys.

Contents

Introduction

One way in which we improve the quality of our lives is to surround ourselves with things we enjoy looking at and caring for. The projects in this book promise to help make your home, yard, and workplace reflect your personal style and interests. You may even want to try constructing some of the wood pieces, which can be very rewarding and give added meaning to the finished piece. It is so fulfilling to create a work of your own from a pine board—to give it form and function, to decorate it, and then to display and use it or give it as a special gift to a dear one. This book is intended for that purpose—to help you create wonderful decorative and functional pieces.

Preparing this, my first book, has been an exhausting—and very rewarding—experience. I wanted to provide you with the best instructions and the most enduring designs. I hope you find the book easy to use and in ten years find the pieces you completed still as wonderful and useful as they were when you finished them.

I also wanted to tell you everything about painting that I could, so that you can continue after you've completed the projects in this book to develop your talents further. I believe that though the styles we crafters develop are as varied and personal as our favorite palettes, the underlying motivation is the same—a desire to create lovely, interesting accessories that enrich our homes and lives.

The colors you use are an important element of the personality and character of each piece and will, in most cases, reflect your own personality and taste. I have provided my own selections of color groups for each project—but feel free to experiment and test your creativity.

I use simple, easy-to-follow directions and uncomplicated and helpful painting patterns that will allow you, in a short time, to create a piece that will brighten a corner, or decorate a Christmas tree. I refer to the method used to paint these pieces as "colorbook" painting or, in other words, Folk Art—the art of the common or untrained person. Folk Art is the spirit of the moment, whatever you wish to create.

Follow my designs or create your own. Start at the beginning of the book or skip around. Whichever you do, do it with a light heart and the joy of creativity. Whenever you complete a piece, be sure to sign and date it. This will truly mark your work as hand-crafted, one-of-a-kind folk art, increasing its value over time, as well as adding to its personal significance.

One special note: It's very important to read the General Instructions and Basic Procedures for all projects, beginning on page 200. This information is critical to a successful project, with particular regard to drying time and finishes. If you have any questions concerning any aspect of this book, please feel free to contact me. I'll probably be working in the shop, painting a new project.

Marina Alexee Grant

Welcome to Country

Changing Seasons Welcome Signs

*This group of seasonal welcome signs is a charming way
to greet each changing season and each visitor who comes to call.*

MATERIALS

Wooden seasonal welcome kit
Sandpaper
Tack cloth
Sealer
Paper towels
Acrylic palette pad
Palette knife
Water containers
Small piece of natural sponge
Linseed oil/mineral spirits
Brown stain
Antiquing mud (4-oz. jar) *or* Burnt Umber oil paint
1″ polyfoam sponge brush
Scruffy old toothbrush *or* stencil brush
Brushes: #1 *or* #2 round; #3 round; #8 *or* #10 flat

Pencil *or* marking pen
Graphite paper
White transfer paper
Tracing paper
Drafting tape
Stylus
Eraser
Steel wool
Varnish
Phillips screwdriver
Pliers
Wood glue *or* glue gun (optional)
Paste wax

PALETTE

Delta Ceramcoat	*Jo Sonja Chroma*	*Illinois Bronze*
Antique White	Warm White	Antique White
Raw Sienna	Raw Sienna	Tumbleweed
Black	Carbon Black	Soft Black
Bright Red	Napthol Red Light	Jo Sonja Red
Vintage Wine	★	★
Blue Haze	★	★
Empire Gold	Turner's Yellow	Dijon Gold
Georgia Clay	Norwegian Orange	Pennsylvania Clay
Woodland Night	★	Prairie Green
Wedgewood Green	Jade	Village Green

Note: If you are going to hang the signs so that both
sides are visible, you might want to consider painting
both sides.

DIRECTIONS

To prepare for this project, please read and follow the General Instructions and Basic Procedures for all projects (beginning on page 200) and the instructions for those particular Special Techniques used in this project (beginning on page 206).

1. Assemble hanger per kit instructions, using screws (and glue, if you wish).
2. Stain hanger and button plugs brown.
3. Transfer the word WELCOME.
4. Mix 6 parts Antique White, ½ part Tumbleweed, and ⅛ part Dijon Gold and use mixture to paint the word WELCOME. (Save this mixture to use later in the project.)
5. Apply spattering to entire piece—first using Soft Black and then Antique White.
6. Attach metal hangers.
7. Finish hanger and plugs with 3 or 4 thin coats of varnish.
8. Apply at least 2 coats of paste wax.
9. Use screws to attach hanger where you want to display it permanently.
10. Tap in button plugs.

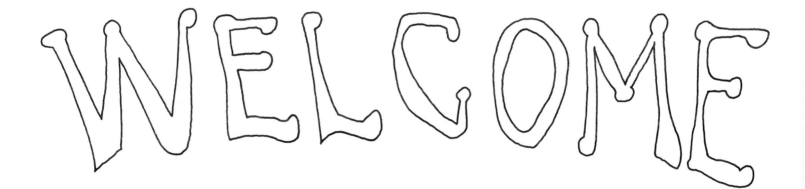

❧❧❧ **Spring Sign** ❧❧❧

*For me, spring evokes memories of strawberries and the
annual Mother-Daughter Banquet held at our local church
the Saturday before Mother's Day. Traditionally, we
topped off this feast with the most delicious strawberry
shortcake. It was always fun, hulling and sugaring the berries,
and then whipping and baking the ingredients for three hundred
shortcakes. Maybe, as you paint this spring welcome sign, you'll
take a break to make a shortcake. Shown, page 7.*

❧❧❧

DIRECTIONS

To prepare for this project, please read and follow the General Instructions and Basic Procedures for all projects (beginning on page 200) and the instructions for those particular Special Techniques used in this project (beginning on page 206).

Paint the Heart and Banner

1. Paint heart and banner in Antique White.
2. Shade banner in Tumbleweed.

Transfer and Paint the Decorative Details

1. Transfer and paint the word SPRING in Prairie Green.
2. Transfer general outline and large leaves.
3. Paint large leaves in Prairie Green.
4. Shade behind the leaves onto heart in Tumbleweed.
5. Transfer veins onto leaves.
6. Mix 1 part Dijon Gold, 1 part Tumbleweed, and 1 part Antique White and use mixture to paint veins in leaves.
7. Shade leaves in Soft Black to separate them.
8. Transfer berries and lined leaves.

9. Paint berries in Jo Sonja Red. (You may need to apply 4 or 5 coats to obtain good coverage.)
10. Paint seeds in Dijon Gold.
11. Mix 1 part Jo Sonja Red and 1 part Vintage Wine and use mixture to shade berries.
12. Paint lined leaves in Soft Black.
13. Mix 1 part Antique White and 1 part Jo Sonja Red and use mixture to paint roses.
14. Mix 2 parts Jo Sonja Red and ½ part Vintage Wine and use mixture to shade roses.
15. Transfer remaining elements of pattern.
16. Paint daisy petals in Antique White.
17. Paint daisy centers in Dijon Gold.
18. Paint calyx on berries in Village Green.

Complete the Finishing Touches

1. Apply spattering—first using Soft Black, then Antique White, and then Prairie Green.
2. Apply antiquing mud. Allow to dry completely, at least 24 hours.
3. Attach screw eyes.
4. Finish with at least 4 thin coats of varnish.
5. Apply at least 2 coats of paste wax.

SCREW EYE

VEINS

SPRING

SHADE

12

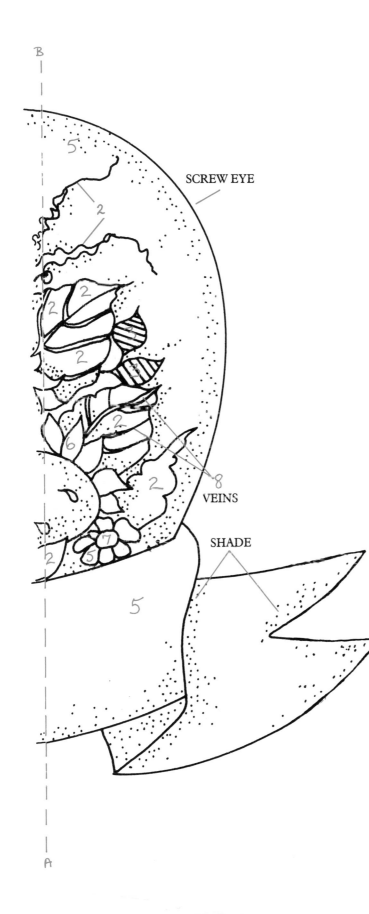

SCREW EYE

VEINS

SHADE

SPRING SIGN
1 TUMBLEWEED
2 PRAIRIE GREEN
3 SOFT BLACK
4 JO SONJA RED
5 ANTIQUE WHITE
6 VILLAGE GREEN
7 DIJON GOLD

Mixtures
8 DIJON GOLD + TUMBLEWEED
  + ANTIQUE WHITE
9 ANTIQUE WHITE + JO SONJA RED
10 JO SONJA RED + VINTAGE WINE

13

Summer Sign

*Picnics, craft fairs, farm markets, hammocks, green grass,
lawn sprinklers, kids at play, flowers in bloom, porch swings,
Fourth of July parades, watermelons sold from a road stand—
the sights of sunny summer are all the inspiration
you need to paint this welcome sign.*

DIRECTIONS

To prepare for this project, please read and follow the General Instructions and Basic Procedures for all projects (beginning on page 200) and the instructions for those particular Special Techniques used in this project (beginning on page 206).

Transfer and Paint Melon

1. Transfer general outline to melon and SUMMER to banner attachment.
2. Mix 4 parts Jo Sonja Red and ½ part Antique White and use mixture to paint the meat of the melon. Apply with a sponge brush, using short, choppy strokes. Don't strive for a perfect curve line.
3. Paint rind in Antique White using same method as in step 2. Let a fuzzy line remain where meat and rind meet.
4. Using Prairie Green, paint a ¼-inch band into the white curve of rind and onto entire underside of piece.
5. Add a bit of Village Green to rind, using a sponge to give a mottled effect.
6. Transfer seeds.
7. Paint seeds in Soft Black.
8. Mix ½ part Jo Sonja Red and ½ part Vintage Wine and using Floated Color technique randomly shade around seeds.

Paint Banner

1. Mix 5 parts Blue Haze and 1½ parts Antique White and use mixture to paint banner.
2. Using Floated Color technique, shade around outside edge of banner with Blue Haze.
3. Mix 1 part Soft Black and 1 part Blue Haze and using Floated Color technique, shade and create the creases in the banner. If desired, use a liner brush and the same color to define the creases.
4. Apply spattering to both pieces—first using Antique White and then Soft Black.
5. Using mixture from step 4 of "Hanger," paint the word SUMMER on the banner.

Paint the Birds

1. Paint birds in Soft Black.
2. Mix 1 part Dijon Gold and 1 part Pennsylvania Clay and use mixture to paint bird beaks.
3. Use mixture from step 4 of "Hanger" to paint bird eyes.

Complete the Finishing Touches

1. Using Antique White, apply spattering to all the pieces.
2. Apply antiquing mud. Allow to dry completely, at least 24 hours.
3. Attach screw eyes.
4. Finish with at least 4 thin coats of varnish.
5. Apply at least 2 coats of paste wax.

Clockwise from left above: Summer Sign, Fall Sign, Happy Holidays Sign

SUMMER SIGN
1 SOFT BLACK
2 ANTIQUE WHITE
3 PRAIRIE GREEN
4 VILLAGE GREEN
5 BLUE HAZE

Mixtures
6 ANTIQUE WHITE + TUMBLEWEED
   + DIJON GOLD
7 JO SONJA RED + ANTIQUE WHITE
8 JO SONJA RED + VINTAGE WINE
9 BLUE HAZE + ANTIQUE WHITE
10 SOFT BLACK + BLUE HAZE
11 PENNSYLVANIA CLAY + DIJON GOLD

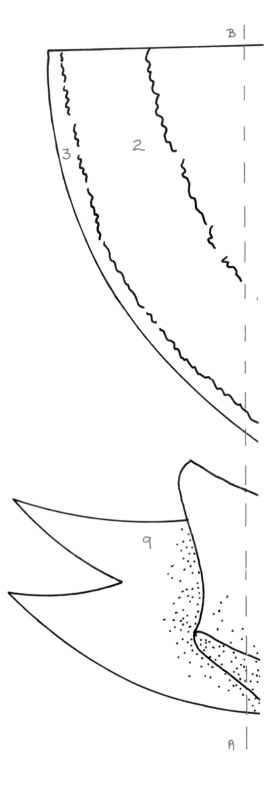

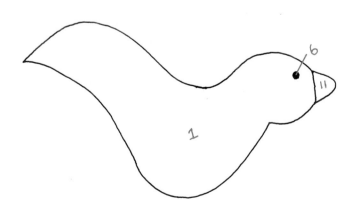

SHADE

17

Fall Harvest Sign

I like the idea of combining a jack-o'-lantern pumpkin and the fruits of the field, the abundant harvest will remind visitors and family that Halloween goodies and Thanksgiving bounty are at hand. Shown, page 15.

DIRECTIONS

To prepare for this project, please read and follow the General Instructions and Basic Procedures for all projects (beginning on page 200) and the instructions for those particular Special Techniques used in this project (beginning on page 206).

Paint the Pumpkin and Banner

1. Transfer general outline to pumpkin and FALL HARVEST to banner.
2. Mix 5 parts Pennsylvania Clay and 2 parts Dijon Gold and use mixture to paint pumpkin. (Save some of this mixture to use later in the project.)
3. Using mixture from step 4 of "Hanger," paint banner.
4. Shade banner in Tumbleweed as indicated on the pattern.
5. Mix 2 parts Prairie Green, ½ part Tumbleweed, and ½ part Dijon Gold and use mixture to paint the words FALL HARVEST on the banner. (Save this mixture to use later in the project.)
6. Using Floated Color technique, apply Dijon Gold to the pumpkin near the center. (Look at the photograph and apply the paint as needed to obtain the depth of color desired.)
7. Shade pumpkin in Tumbleweed as indicated on the pattern.

Decorate the Pumpkin

1. Transfer details of pumpkin.
2. Paint eyes, nose, and mouth in Soft Black.
3. Outline one side of the eyes, nose, and mouth in Dijon Gold. (Refer to photo.)

4. Outline the Dijon Gold outline in a very thin line of Jo Sonja Red.

Paint the Leaves and Harvest

1. Transfer the leaves, fruits, and vegetables.
2. Using Tumbleweed, shade heavily under the grapes and leaves.
3. Using mixture from step 5 of "Paint the Pumpkin and Banner," paint leaves.
4. Transfer veins.
5. Paint veins in Soft Black.
6. Outline 1 side of leaves and 1 side of veins in Village Green.
7. Using mixture from step 2 of "Paint the Pumpkin and Banner," paint the orange.
8. Shade orange in Tumbleweed.
9. Mix 2 parts Dijon Gold and ½ part Antique White and use mixture to paint 1 apple yellow.
10. Shade yellow apple in Tumbleweed.
11. Mix 2 parts Prairie Green, 1 part Dijon Gold, and ¼ part Antique White and use mixture to paint 1 apple green.
12. Mix 1 part Prairie Green and ¼ part Soft Black and use mixture to shade green apple.
13. Mix 2 parts Jo Sonja Red and ¼ part Vintage Wine and use mixture to paint 1 apple red.
14. Dampen apples with brush and then highlight with a bit of Antique White using Side-Loaded technique.
15. Shade red apple in Vintage Wine.
16. Paint the stems of the yellow, green, and red apples in Soft Black.

17. Mix 2 parts Jo Sonja Red and 2 parts Vintage Wine and use mixture to paint eggplant.
18. Mix ¼ part Vintage Wine, ¼ part Soft Black, and ¼ part Jo Sonja Red and use mixture to shade eggplant, using Floated Color technique.
19. Mix 1 part Village Green, 1 part Dijon Gold, and ½ part Tumbleweed and use mixture to paint eggplant stem.
20. Shade eggplant stem in Soft Black.
21. Highlight eggplant stem in Antique White.
22. Dampen eggplant and apply mixture of ½ part Vintage Wine, ½ part Jo Sonja Red, and ½ part Antique White to highlight, using Side-Loaded technique.
23. Mix 3 parts Jo Sonja Red, 3 parts Vintage Wine, and 1 part Antique White and use mixture to paint grapes. Let dry.
24. Repeat step 23 above, applying more grapes so that some overlap the first bunch.
25. Shade 1 side of the grapes in Vintage Wine.
26. Mix ¼ part Jo Sonja Red, ¼ part Vintage Wine, and ¼ part Antique White and use mixture to highlight other side of the grapes.

Complete the Finishing Touches
1. Apply spattering—first using Soft Black, then Antique White, and then Tumbleweed.
2. Apply antiquing mud. Allow to dry completely, at least 24 hours.
3. Attach screw eyes.
4. Finish with 3 or 4 thin coats of varnish.
5. Apply at least 2 coats of paste wax.

❧❧❧ Happy Holidays Sign ❧❧❧

This snowman carries winter's message of Happy Holidays.
Display him through the season until mid-February
or whenever the last snowflake falls. Shown, page 15.

❧❧❧

DIRECTIONS
To prepare for this project, please read and follow the General Instructions and Basic Procedures for all projects (beginning on page 200) and the instructions for those particular Special Techniques used in this project (beginning on page 206).

Paint Snowman and Banner
1. Transfer hat line onto snowman.
2. Paint snowman in Antique White.
3. Paint banner and hat in Jo Sonja Red.
4. Mix 1 part Jo Sonja Red and ¼ part Prairie Green and use mixture to shade hat and banner.
5. Transfer and paint the words HAPPY HOLIDAYS in Antique White on the banner.

Transfer and Paint the Details
1. Transfer details onto snowman.
2. Paint eyes, mouth, and buttons in Soft Black.
3. Mix 1 part Pennsylvania Clay and 1 part Dijon Gold and use mixture to paint nose.
4. Shade nose and body in Tumbleweed.

Complete the Finishing Touches
1. Apply spattering—first using Black, then Antique White, and then Prairie Green.
2. Apply antiquing mud. Allow to dry completely, at least 24 hours.
3. Attach screw eyes.
4. Finish with 3 or 4 thin coats of varnish.
5. Apply at least 2 coats of paste wax.
6. Add, if you wish, an old piece of doily or crocheted material as a scarf.

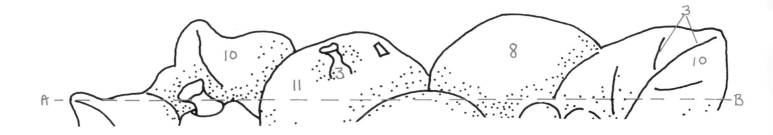

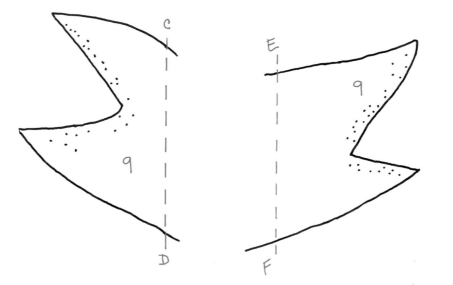

FALL HARVEST SIGN
1   TUMBLEWEED
2   DIJON GOLD
3   SOFT BLACK
4   JO SONJA RED
5   VILLAGE GREEN
6   VINTAGE WINE
7   ANTIQUE WHITE

Mixtures
 8   PENNSYLVANIA CLAY + DIJON GOLD
 9   ANTIQUE WHITE + TUMBLEWEED + DIJON GOLD
10   PRAIRIE GREEN + TUMBLEWEED + DIJON GOLD
11   DIJON GOLD + ANTIQUE WHITE
12   TUMBLEWEED + SOFT BLACK
13   PRAIRIE GREEN + DIJON GOLD + ANTIQUE WHITE
14   JO SONJA RED + VINTAGE WINE
15   VINTAGE WINE + SOFT BLACK + JO SONJA RED
16   JO SONJA RED + VINTAGE WINE + ANTIQUE WHITE
17   VILLAGE GREEN + DIJON GOLD + TUMBLEWEED

HAPPY HOLIDAYS SIGN
1 ANTIQUE WHITE
2 JO SONJA RED
3 SOFT BLACK
4 TUMBLEWEED

Mixtures
5 JO SONJA RED + PRAIRIE GREEN
6 PENNSYLVANIA CLAY + DIJON GOLD

22

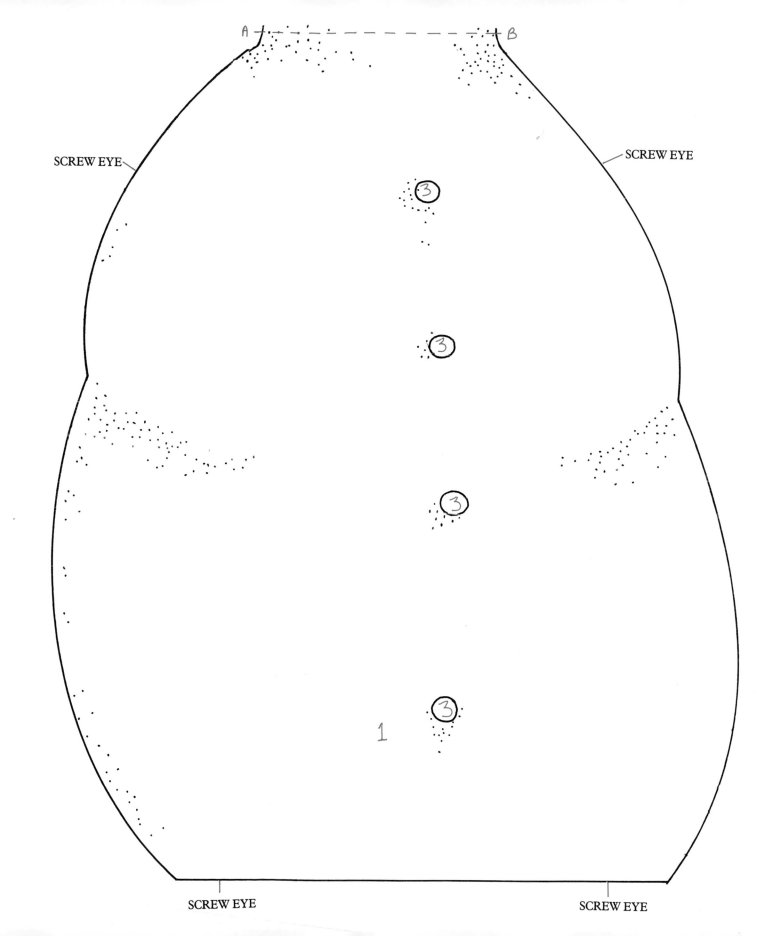

A   B

SCREW EYE   SCREW EYE

③

③

③

③

1

SCREW EYE   SCREW EYE

Country Nooks
and Crannies

Country Candle Box

This is one of those early American pieces that you see in museums and restored homes around the country. Long ago, this type of box was used to keep candles handy since they were needed after the sun went down. These days, it could be filled with notes, small collectibles, or perhaps dried flowers.

MATERIALS

Wooden candle box
Sandpaper
Tack cloth
Sealer
Paper towels
Acrylic palette pad
Palette knife
Water containers
1″ polyfoam sponge brushes (2)
Antiquing mud (4-oz. jar) *or* Burnt Umber oil paint
Linseed oil/mineral spirits
Brushes: #6 *or* #8 flat; #3 round; #1 round liner

Pencil *or* marking pen
Graphite paper
Tracing paper
Drafting tape
Stylus
Eraser
Steel wool
Varnish

PALETTE

Delta Ceramcoat	*Jo Sonja Chroma*	*Illinois Bronze*
Dresden Flesh	★	★
Liberty Blue	★	★
Dusty Purple	★	
Adobe	Rose Pink	Wineberry
		Brick

DIRECTIONS

To prepare for this project, please read and follow the General Instructions and Basic Procedures for all projects (beginning on page 200) and the instructions for those particular Special Techniques used in this project (beginning on page 206).

Paint the Box

1. Paint the inside of the box in Liberty Blue. (Refer to drawing A.)
2. Paint the outside of the box in Dresden Flesh.
3. Paint the ¾″-wide edges at the top and sides of the box in Dusty Purple.

4. Apply Rose Pink dots at ¾" intervals to the Dusty Purple edges.
5. Transfer margins to front face of box. (Refer to drawing B.)
6. Paint the margins in Liberty Blue.
7. Transfer stripes to these margins.
8. Paint the stripes in Rose Pink and Dusty Purple, alternating colors.
9. Paint the line following the contours on the front face and inside face in Dusty Purple.

Transfer and Paint the Side Designs
1. Transfer leaf design to left and right sides of box. (Refer to drawing C.)
2. Paint leaf design in Dusty Purple.
3. Transfer the margins to each side of the leaf design.
4. Paint these margins in Dusty Purple.
5. Transfer the zigzag lines to the margins.
6. Paint the zigzag lines in Liberty Blue and Rose Pink, alternating colors.

Transfer and Paint the Inside Face Design
1. Transfer the stems, leaves, and hearts to the inside face of the box, aligning the hole in the center of the heart with the hole in the candle box. (Refer to drawing D.)
2. Paint the stems and leaves in Dresden Flesh.
3. Paint the hearts in Rose Pink.
4. Outline the hearts in Dusty Purple.

Transfer and Paint the Front Face Design
1. Transfer the vases and their contents to the left and right of the center dip on the front face of the box. (Refer to drawing E.)
2. Paint the vases and the bar under the vases in Liberty Blue.
3. Paint the leaves and stems in Dusty Purple.
4. Paint the hearts in Rose Pink.
5. Outline each Rose Pink heart in Dusty Purple.

Complete the Finishing Touches
1. Sand the box to age it.
2. Apply antiquing mud. Allow to dry completely, at least 24 hours.
3. Finish with 2 thin coats of varnish.

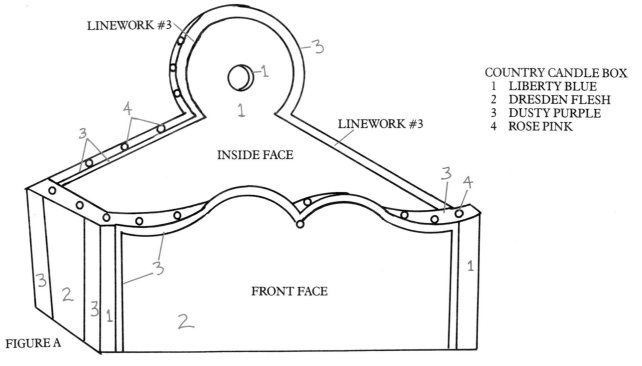

LINEWORK #3

LINEWORK #3

INSIDE FACE

FRONT FACE

COUNTRY CANDLE BOX
1 LIBERTY BLUE
2 DRESDEN FLESH
3 DUSTY PURPLE
4 ROSE PINK

FIGURE A

FIGURE B

THIS EDGE TOWARD OUTSIDE OF BOX

4
1
3
3

FIGURE C

2
4
1
3
3
3
3
1
4

FIGURE E

4
4
3
4
OUTLINE
3
4
1
1

FIGURE D

4
LINE UP WITH
BOX HOLE
2
OUTLINE
3
4
4
2
2

Schoolhouse Lap Desk

Lap desks have been around since shortly after the creation of the feather pen, I have been told, and although the lap-top computer has now replaced the lap desk for many of us, the desk remains a favorite decorating piece and is wonderful if you have an occasion to spend the day in bed.

MATERIALS

Wooden lap desk
Sandpaper
Tack cloth
Sealer
Paper towels
Acrylic palette pad
Palette knife
Water containers
1″ polyfoam sponge brush
Linseed oil
Mineral spirits
Antiquing mud (4-oz. jar) *or* Burnt Umber oil paint
Brushes: #10 flat; #1 and #3 round; large fan brush

Pencil *or* marking pen
Graphite paper
Tracing paper
Drafting tape
Stylus
Eraser
Steel wool
Varnish

PALETTE

Delta Ceramcoat	*Jo Sonja Chroma*	*Illinois Bronze*
White	Titanium White	White Wash
★	★	Light Soft Blue
Black	Carbon Black	Soft Black
Green Isle	Brilliant Green	Holiday Green
Raw Sienna	Raw Sienna	Tumbleweed
Straw	★	Golden Harvest
Burnt Umber	Brown Earth	Burnt Umber
Bright Red	Napthol Red Light	Jo Sonja Red

DIRECTIONS

To prepare for this project, please read and follow the General Instructions and Basic Procedures for all projects (beginning on page 200) and the instructions for those particular Special Techniques used in this project (beginning on page 206).

Transfer and Paint the Design

1. Paint all outside surfaces of the desk in White Wash. (The inside, the bottom of the lid, and the bottom of the desk will be stained later.)
2. Paint striping around the lid and bottom in Light Soft Blue. (Refer to photo.)
3. Transfer oval scene (inset) and oval band outline.
4. Paint sky in Light Soft Blue.
5. Dampen sky with water before applying clouds (Step 6).
6. Dip little finger in White Wash so that only a sparse amount remains on your finger and apply clouds. (I dip my finger into the paint and practice on paper. When I think that the clouds look light and airy, I apply them to the painted and dampened surface.)
7. Mix 2 parts Golden Harvest, 2 parts Holiday Green, ⅛ part Soft Black, and ¼ part Tumbleweed and use mixture to paint grass.
8. Transfer house and trees.
9. Mix 3 parts Golden Harvest, 2 parts Holiday Green, and ¼ part Tumbleweed and use mixture to paint trees.
10. Dampen trees and apply Golden Harvest to one side of each tree. (Refer to photo.)
11. Paint house in Tumbleweed.
12. Paint roof in Burnt Umber.
13. Paint chimneys in Soft Black.
14. Transfer windows and doors.
15. Paint door in Jo Sonja Red.
16. Paint windowpanes in Soft Black.
17. Paint window frames in Tumbleweed.
18. Outline door in Soft Black.
19. Using large fan brush, apply Golden Harvest to grass. (Refer to photo.)
20. Transfer fence.
21. Paint fence in Soft Black.

Paint the Oval Band and Corner Tulips

1. Paint oval band in Golden Harvest.
2. Transfer floral details to Golden Harvest band and to bottom right and left corners of desk.
3. Mix 3 parts Holiday Green, 3 parts Golden Harvest, and ⅛ part Jo Sonja Red and use mixture to paint leaves on band green. (Save this mixture to use later in the project.)
4. Shade each leaf at stem origin in Soft Black.
5. Paint veins in Soft Black.
6. Paint tulips and buds in Jo Sonja Red. Be sure to paint the tulips in the bottom corners.
7. Using mixture from step 3 above, paint tulip leaves.
8. Add dot in Golden Harvest to opening of each tulip.
9. Add dot design in Jo Sonja Red among the greens.
10. Add a dot in Golden Harvest to each bud on the 4 red flowers at the top of the oval design.

Transfer and Paint Lettering

1. Transfer lettering.
2. Paint lettering in Burnt Umber.

Complete the Finishing Touches

1. Outline the outside edge of the oval band in Burnt Umber.
2. Spatter the outside surfaces in Burnt Umber.
3. Mix 2 tablespoons of antiquing solution, 2 tablespoons of mineral spirits, and ⅛ teaspoon of linseed oil and use the mixture to stain the inside, the bottom, and the underside of the lid.
4. Apply antiquing mud. Allow to dry completely, at least 24 hours.
5. Finish with 2 or 3 thin coats of varnish.

a b c d e f g h i j k l

m n o p q r s t

ALL LETTERING #7

LEFT BOTTOM CORNER

RIGHT BOTTOM CORNER

SCHOOLHOUSE LAP DESK
1 WHITE WASH
2 LIGHT SOFT BLUE
3 HOLIDAY GREEN
4 SOFT BLACK
5 TUMBLEWEED
6 GOLDEN HARVEST
7 BURNT UMBER
8 JO SONJA RED

Mixtures
9 GOLDEN HARVEST + HOLIDAY GREEN + SOFT BLACK + TUMBLEWEED
10 GOLDEN HARVEST + HOLIDAY GREEN + TUMBLEWEED
11 HOLIDAY GREEN + GOLDEN HARVEST + JO SONJA RED

31

7 OUTLINE

32

Strawberry Charm Boxes

This group sits on a shelf or desk and will hold a variety of small items, such as stamps or paper clips. These boxes are quick and easy to paint and make good gift items and great little organizers. Shown, page 29.

MATERIALS

Wooden box set
Sandpaper
Tack cloth
Sealer
Paper towels
Acrylic palette pad
Palette knife
Water containers
Antiquing mud (4-oz. jar) *or* Burnt Umber oil paint
Linseed oil/mineral spirits
Brushes: #1 round; #3 round; #8 flat

Pencil *or* marking pen
Graphite paper
Tracing paper
Drafting tape
Stylus
Eraser
Steel wool
Varnish

PALETTE

Delta Ceramcoat	*Jo Sonja Chroma*	*Illinois Bronze*
Cape Cod + White	French Blue + Titanium White	Light Stoneware Blue
Bright Red	Napthol Red Light	Jo Sonja Red
★	★	Purple Canyon
		True Orange
Pumpkin	★	Golden Harvest
Straw	Yellow Oxide + White	Prairie Green
Woodland Night	★	

DIRECTIONS

To prepare for this project, please read and follow the General Instructions and Basic Procedures for all projects (beginning on page 200) and the instructions for those particular Special Techniques used in this project (beginning on page 206).

Paint the Boxes

1. Paint each box in Light Stoneware Blue.
2. Transfer berry design or flower and stripe design.
3. Paint berries in Jo Sonja Red.
4. Shade berries in Purple Canyon.
5. Highlight opposite side of berries in True Orange.
6. Transfer seeds and leaf designs to berries.

7. Paint seeds in Golden Harvest.
8. Paint leaf designs in Prairie Green.
9. Paint flower center in Golden Harvest.
10. Paint "petal" dots in Jo Sonja Red.
11. Paint the stems and leaves in Prairie Green.
12. Paint the top and bottom rims of 3 boxes in Jo Sonja Red. (Refer to photo.)

Paint the Lids
1. Paint the lids Light Stoneware Blue.
2. Transfer berry and floral designs to the lids.
3. Paint all leaves and floral accent dots in Prairie Green.

4. Paint berry on one lid and flower center on stamp box lid in Jo Sonja Red.
5. Paint berry seeds in Golden Harvest.
6. Paint "petal" dots on stamp box lid in True Orange.

Complete the Finishing Touches
1. Apply antiquing mud to boxes and lids. Allow to dry completely, at least 24 hours.
2. Finish with 2 thin coats of varnish.

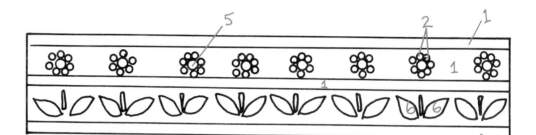

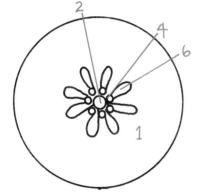

STRAWBERRY CHARM BOXES
1 LIGHT STONEWARE BLUE
2 JO SONJA RED
3 PURPLE CANYON
4 TRUE ORANGE
5 GOLDEN HARVEST
6 PRAIRIE GREEN

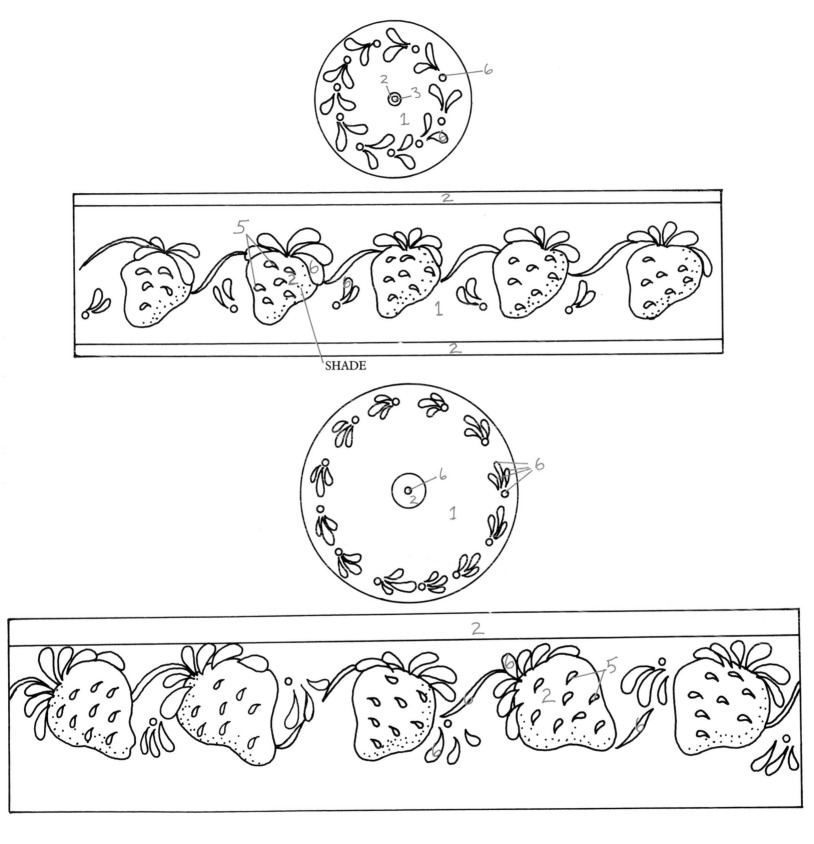

SHADE

Folk Angel from Heaven

This angel was designed in the 1880s and has grown in popularity ever since. She can be displayed year-round, singly or in a group, and makes a wonderful focal point for a Christmas vignette. Ours is currently hanging in our bedroom and gets our day off to a heavenly start.

MATERIALS

Wooden angel
Sandpaper
Tack cloth
Sealer
Paper towels
Acrylic palette pad
Palette knife
Water containers
Antiquing mud (4-oz. jar) *or* Burnt Umber oil paint
Linseed oil/mineral spirits
1″ polyfoam sponge brush (2)
Brushes: #1 *or* #3 round; #8 *or* #10 flat

Pencil *or* marking pen
Graphite paper
Tracing paper
Drafting tape
Stylus
Eraser
Steel wool
Varnish

PALETTE

Delta Ceramcoat	*Jo Sonja Chroma*	*Illinois Bronze*
Medium Flesh	★	Peaches n' Cream
Burnt Umber	Brown Earth	Burnt Umber
Straw	Yellow Oxide + Titanium White	Golden Harvest
Black	Carbon Black	Soft Black
Maple Sugar	★	Devonshire Cream
Salem Green	Teal Green + White	Telemark Green
Coral + White	★	Light Coral Belles
★	★	Light Soft Blue
Mendocino	Burgundy	Bordeaux
Bright Red	Napthol Red Light	Jo Sonja Red
Burnt Sienna	Burnt Sienna	Burnt Sienna
Ivory	Titanium White	White Wash

DIRECTIONS

To prepare for this project, please read and follow the General Instructions and Basic Procedures for all projects (beginning on page 200) and the instructions for those particular Special Techniques used in this project (beginning on page 206).

Transfer and Paint Angel

1. Transfer outline of face, hand, hair, gown, and slippers.
2. Paint face and hand in Peaches n' Cream.
3. Paint pinafore in Devonshire Cream.
4. Paint gown and sleeve in Light Soft Blue.

Paint Horn

1. Paint horn in Burnt Umber.
2. Apply crosshatch strokes to thickest section of horn in Golden Harvest. (Refer to photo.)
3. Mix 1 part Soft Black and 1 part Burnt Umber and use mixture to shade horn.

Transfer and Paint Floral Design

1. Transfer floral details to angel's gown.
2. Mix 2 parts Telemark Green and 2 parts Golden Harvest and use mixture to paint stems and most of the leaves. (Refer to photo and next step.)
3. Mix 1 part Soft Black and 1 part Telemark Green and use mixture to paint a few leaves for accent. (These leaves are not filled in the pattern.)
4. Using mixture from step 2 above, complete floral linework.
5. Mix 2½ parts Light Coral Belles, 2½ parts Bordeaux, and ½ part Jo Sonja Red and use mixture to paint all the flowers.
6. Outline the flowers in Bordeaux.
7. Add dots to flower petals in Bordeaux.
8. Apply random dots in Bordeaux, Light Soft Blue, and Telemark Green throughout the floral design.

Paint the Angel's Face and Hair

1. Mix 1 part Jo Sonja Red and ⅛ part Light Coral Belles and use mixture and Dry Brush Color technique to paint angel's cheek.
2. Using the mixture from step 1 above, paint the lips.

3. Outline lips in Jo Sonja Red.
4. Paint hair in Burnt Umber.
5. Add a few strokes to hair in Burnt Sienna.
6. Add a few strokes to hair in Golden Harvest.
7. Transfer hair band.
8. Paint hair band in Devonshire Cream.
9. Paint hair band in Light Soft Blue (over Devonshire Cream).
10. Transfer details of face.
11. Paint eyebrow in Burnt Umber.
12. Paint white of eye in White Wash.
13. Outline entire upper and lower eyelids in Burnt Umber.
14. Shade eyelid in Burnt Umber.
15. Paint iris of eye in Light Soft Blue.
16. Outline iris in Burnt Umber.
17. Paint pupil in Soft Black.
18. Mix ½ part Burnt Umber and ½ part Soft Black and use mixture to paint eyelashes.

Paint Slippers and Stockings

1. Mix 1½ part Soft Black and ½ part Burnt Umber and use mixture to paint stockings.
2. Add stripes to stockings in Golden Harvest.
3. Paint slippers in Burnt Umber.
4. Paint soles of slippers in Soft Black.

Complete the Finishing Touches

1. Mix ½ part Burnt Sienna and ⅛ part Burnt Umber and use mixture to shade face, hands, and pinafore.
2. Shade blue gown in Burnt Sienna.
3. Apply antiquing mud. Allow to dry completely, at least 24 hours.
4. Using Outline-and-Paint technique, add veins to all light leaves in Light Soft Blue.
5. Using Outline-and-Paint technique, highlight hair band in Light Soft Blue.
6. Using Outline-and-Paint technique, apply a small amount of Light Soft Blue at sleeve edges and along hem of gown. Blend with your finger.
7. Using Outline-and-Paint technique, highlight hair in Burnt Sienna.
8. Using Outline-and-Paint technique, highlight hair in Golden Harvest.

9. Using Outline-and-Paint technique and mixture from step 5 of "Transfer and Paint Floral Design," highlight flowers at random.

10. Using Outline-and-Paint technique, highlight horn with Light Soft Blue. Use finger to blend.

11. Finish with 2 thin coats of varnish.

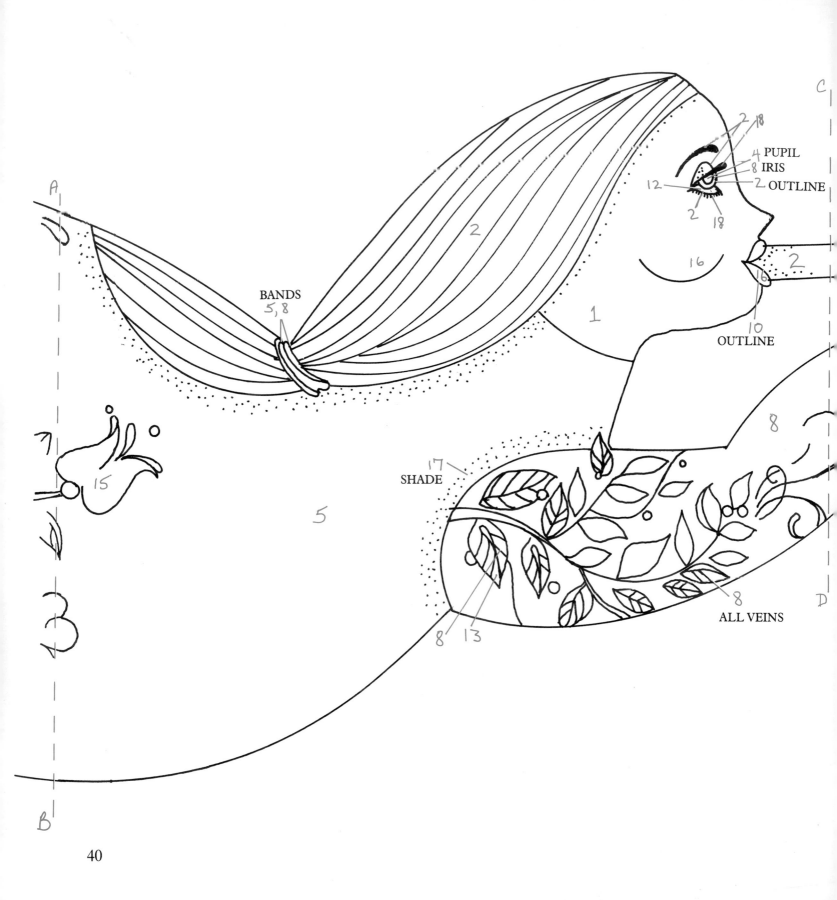

BANDS
5, 8

2 18
4 PUPIL
8 IRIS
12 2 OUTLINE
2 18

16
2
16

1
10
OUTLINE

8

SHADE
17

ALL VEINS
8

8 13

7
15

5

40

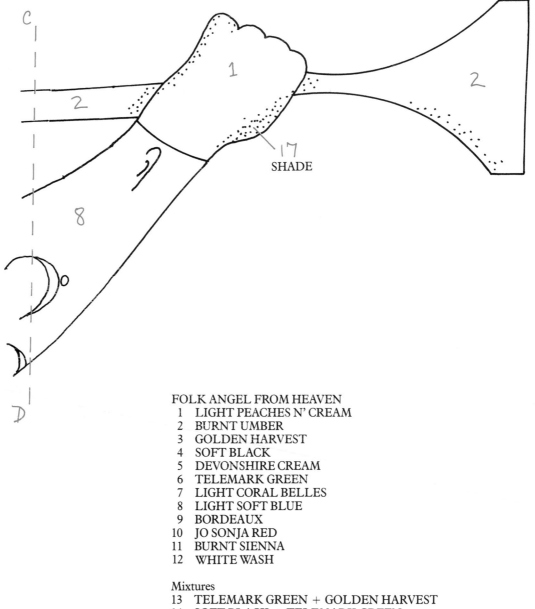

SHADE

FOLK ANGEL FROM HEAVEN
1 LIGHT PEACHES N' CREAM
2 BURNT UMBER
3 GOLDEN HARVEST
4 SOFT BLACK
5 DEVONSHIRE CREAM
6 TELEMARK GREEN
7 LIGHT CORAL BELLES
8 LIGHT SOFT BLUE
9 BORDEAUX
10 JO SONJA RED
11 BURNT SIENNA
12 WHITE WASH

Mixtures
13 TELEMARK GREEN + GOLDEN HARVEST
14 SOFT BLACK + TELEMARK GREEN
15 LIGHT CORAL BELLES + BORDEAUX + JO SONJA RED
16 JO SONJA RED + LIGHT CORAL BELLES
17 BURNT SIENNA + BURNT UMBER
18 SOFT BLACK + BURNT UMBER

Marina Blue Birdhouse

This birdhouse should make the most discriminating aviary dweller happy, and it is designed to allow for easy cleaning after each season. I think Audubon would approve.

MATERIALS

Wooden birdhouse
Sandpaper
Tack cloth
Sealer
Paper towels
Acrylic palette pad
Palette knife
Water containers
1" polyfoam sponge brush
Antiquing mud (4-oz. jar) *or* Burnt Umber oil paint
Linseed oil/mineral spirits
Brushes: #4 flat; #2 round

Pencil *or* marking pen
Graphite paper
White transfer paper
Tracing paper
Drafting tape
Stylus
Eraser
Steel wool
Varnish
Paste wax

PALETTE

Delta Ceramcoat	*Jo Sonja Chroma*	*Illinois Bronze*
Colonial Blue	Aqua	Marina Blue
White	Titanium White	Soft White
Georgia Clay	Norwegian Orange	Pennsylvania Clay
Black	Carbon Black	Soft Black

DIRECTIONS

To prepare for this project, please read and follow the General Instructions and Basic Procedures for all projects (beginning on page 200) and the instructions for those particular Special Techniques used in this project (beginning on page 206).

Note: For ease in painting and finishing, remove the two screws holding the base onto the house and separate the pieces.

Paint the Birdhouse
1. Paint the roof, chimney, and base of the birdhouse in Marina Blue.
2. Paint the sides, front, and back in Soft White.
3. Paint the perch, fence rail, and inside rim of the heart in Pennsylvania Clay.

Transfer and Paint the Designs
1. Transfer patterns onto the birdhouse. The hearts on the roof are laid on at 1" intervals across all

rows of the roof. (You can substitute dots for hearts if you wish, but if you do, use the wood end of a brush to apply the dots.)

2. Paint the branches, stems, and leaves in Marina Blue.
3. Paint the flowers, hearts, and rim of the heart-shaped opening in Pennsylvania Clay.
4. Paint the center dots of the flowers in Soft Black.
5. Paint birds in Soft Black.
6. Transfer birds' wings and eyes.
7. Paint birds' wings and eyes in Pennsylvania Clay.

Complete the Finishing Touches

1. Apply antiquing mud. Allow to dry completely, at least 24 hours.
2. Finish with 3 or 4 thin coats of varnish to ensure good coverage and protection from the weather.
3. For outdoor use, apply at least 2 coats of paste wax.
4. Assemble base onto house with screws furnished in kit.

MARINA BLUE BIRDHOUSE
1 MARINA BLUE
2 PENNSYLVANIA CLAY
3 SOFT BLACK

FRONT OF BIRDHOUSE

ALL LINES

44

Pennsylvania Mayflower Bench

The graceful lines and feminine silhouette of this piece
suggest to the romantic at heart that this bench
was perhaps designed by a craftsman in love with a young
woman. Yet it is also practical with a drawer for holding small
treasures. This bench is a reproduction of one that is at least
125 years old. We hope that the craftsman would like this
adaptation of his charming little bench.

MATERIALS

Wooden bench with drawer
Sandpaper
Tack cloth
Sealer
Paper towels
Acrylic palette pad
Palette knife
Water containers
Linseed oil/mineral spirits
1½″ polyfoam sponge brush
Antiquing mud (4-oz. jar) *or* Burnt Umber oil paint
Brushes: #1 *or* #3 round; #8 *or* #10 flat; #3 liner

Pencil *or* marking pen
Graphite paper
Tracing paper
Drafting tape
Stylus
Eraser
Ruler
Steel wool
Varnish

PALETTE

Delta Ceramcoat	*Jo Sonja Chroma*	*Illinois Bronze*
White	Titanium White	White Wash
Bright Red	Napthol Red Light	Jo Sonja Red
Burnt Sienna	Burnt Sienna	Burnt Sienna
Straw	Yellow Oxide	Golden Harvest
Light Chocolate	Fawn	Wicker
Black	Carbon Black	Soft Black
Bittersweet	★	True Orange
Green Isle	★	Holiday Green
Mendocino	Burgundy	Bordeaux

DIRECTIONS

To prepare for this project, please read and follow the General Instructions and Basic Procedures for all projects (beginning on page 200) and the instructions for those particular Special Techniques used in this project (beginning on page 206).

Paint the Bench and Checkerboard

1. Transfer checkerboard design to bench.
2. Mix 12 parts Holiday Green and 2 parts Soft Black and use mixture to paint entire bench, 32 alternating checkerboard squares, and 12 checkers. Remix as needed.
3. Paint the remaining 32 gameboard squares and 12 checkers in Light Chocolate.
4. Paint striping on legs and top surface in Light Chocolate, if you wish. (Refer to photo.)

Transfer and Paint the Tree and Bird Designs

1. Transfer remaining elements of the design to bench.
2. Paint tree trunks in Burnt Sienna.
3. Shade tree trunks in Soft Black.
4. Refer to pattern and paint some of the leaves in Golden Harvest.
5. Paint blank unveined leaves in Soft Black.
6. Paint remaining leaves in Light Chocolate.
7. Paint veins on the Golden Harvest leaves in Jo Sonja Red.
8. Paint veins on Light Chocolate leaves in White Wash.
9. Paint "floral" apples in Jo Sonja Red.
10. Shade "floral" apples in Bordeaux.
11. Add stamen line details to floral apples in Soft Black.
12. Add dots on ends of floral apple stamens in Jo Sonja Red.
13. Add dots to trunk in Jo Sonja Red. (Refer to photo.)
14. Mix 4 parts White Wash, ¼ part Golden Harvest, and ¼ part Light Chocolate and use mixture to paint the birds.
15. Shade birds in Burnt Sienna.
16. Paint the birds' beaks in True Orange.
17. Paint the birds' eyes in Soft Black.

Complete the Finishing Touches

1. Using liner brush, apply scalloped edge detailing in Light Chocolate and White Wash. (Refer to pattern.)
2. Paint drawer knob in Jo Sonja Red.
3. Apply antiquing mud. Allow to dry completely, at least 24 hours.
4. Using Outline-and-Paint technique, highlight along the tree trunk in Light Chocolate, using a slightly wiggling stroke.
5. Using Outline-and-Paint technique, highlight a few leaves with red veins in Jo Sonja Red.
6. Using Outline-and-Paint technique, highlight a few leaves with white veins in White Wash.
7. Using Outline-and-Paint technique, highlight birds' heads, breasts, wings, and tail feathers with White Wash.
8. Using Outline-and-Paint technique, highlight birds' beaks with True Orange.
9. Using Side-Loaded Color technique, highlight a few Light Chocolate gameboard squares in Light Chocolate.
10. Finish bench and checkers with 2 thin coats of varnish.

REPEAT CHECKERBOARD PATTERN FOR A TOTAL OF 8 ROWS OF 8 SQUARES.

PENNSYLVANIA MAYFLOWER BENCH
2 LIGHT CHOCOLATE
3 BURNT SIENNA
4 SOFT BLACK
5 GOLDEN HARVEST
6 JO SONJA RED
7 WHITE WASH
8 BORDEAUX
9 TRUE ORANGE

Mixtures
10 HOLIDAY GREEN + SOFT BLACK
11 WHITE WASH + GOLDEN HARVEST
    + LIGHT CHOCOLATE

49

Folk Hearts Looking Glass

This piece was inspired by three nieces, Jamie, Jessie and Lia,
who sometimes come to call. A few of these girls' favorite
things are my doll collection, glitzy jewelry,
hand-held church bells that ring, pianos, dancing,
our dogs and horses, and the colors pink and purple.

MATERIALS

Wood-framed mirror; heart, tulip and bird
  embellishments
Sandpaper
Tack cloth
Sealer
Paper towels
Acrylic palette pad
Palette knife
Water containers
1″ polyfoam sponge brush (2)
Antiquing mud (4-oz. jar) *or* Burnt Umber oil paint
Linseed oil/mineral spirits
Brushes: #8 *or* #10 round

Pencil *or* marking pen
White transfer paper
Eraser
Steel wool
Varnish
Wood glue *or* glue gun
Embroidery thread
Stapler

PALETTE

Delta Ceramcoat	*Jo Sonja Chroma*	*Illinois Bronze*
Lavender Lace	★	★
Maple Sugar	Opal	★
Woodland Night	★	Prairie Green
★	★	Apache Red
Trail	Fawn + White	Wicker

DIRECTIONS

To prepare for this project, please read and follow the General Instructions and Basic Procedures for all projects (beginning on page 200) and the instructions for those particular Special Techniques used in this project (beginning on page 206).

Paint and Decorate the Frame

1. Paint frame in Lavender Lace.
2. Mix ½ part Maple Sugar, 1¾ parts Apache Red, and ½ part Lavender Lace and use mixture to paint 2 hearts. If you are planning to attach hanging embellishments, use mixture to paint 1 hanging heart.
3. Mix 1½ parts Apache Red and ¼ part Prairie Green and use mixture to paint tulips (and 2 hearts if you are attaching hanging embellishments).
4. Using mixture from step 3 above, add 2 purple dots to top of frame and rows of purple dots to top curve and bottom edge of frame.
5. Paint remaining hearts in Maple Sugar.
6. Using mixture from step 3 above, add dots to Maple Sugar hearts.
7. Add 2 dots on bottom half of frame in Maple Sugar. (Refer to photo.)
8. Mix 1 part Prairie Green and 1 part Lavender Lace and use mixture to paint leaves.
9. Add dot in center of bottom hearts in Wicker.
10. If you are attaching dowel birds and bird hanging embellishments, paint birds in Wicker.

Complete the Finishing Touches

1. If you are attaching glued embellishments, glue pieces onto frame.
2. Apply antiquing mud. Allow to dry completely, at least 24 hours.
3. Finish with 2 thin coats of varnish.
4. Install mirror.
5. If you are attaching hanging embellishments, tie 3 hearts and bird with embroidery thread and staple other end of thread to the back of the frame. (Refer to photo.)

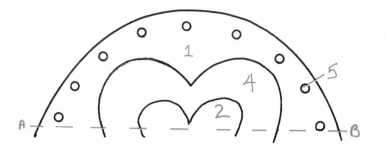

FOLK HEARTS LOOKING GLASS
1   LAVENDER LACE
2   MAPLE SUGAR
3   WICKER

Mixtures
4   MAPLE SUGAR + APACHE RED + LAVENDER LACE
5   APACHE RED + PRAIRIE GREEN
6   PRAIRIE GREEN + LAVENDER LACE

53

Historic Switch Plates

*Decorative switch plates provide an inexpensive and
relatively quick way to add charming detail to a room.
I have discovered that they make excellent gifts
that are enthusiastically received because
most people own the plastic models which,
though functional, are rather plain.*

MATERIALS

Wooden switch plate covers (4)
Sandpaper
Tack cloth
Sealer
Paper towels
Acrylic palette pad
Palette knife
Water containers
1″ polyfoam sponge brush
Antiquing mud (4-oz. jar) *or* Burnt Umber oil paint
Linseed oil/mineral spirits
Brushes: #1 round; #3 round; #8 *or* #10 flat

Pencil *or* marking pen
White transfer paper
Tracing paper
Drafting tape
Stylus
Eraser
Steel wool
Varnish

PALETTE

Delta Ceramcoat	*Jo Sonja Chroma*	*Illinois Bronze*
Antique White	Warm White	Antique White
Black	Carbon Black	Soft Black
Bright Red	Napthol Red Light	Jo Sonja Red
Blue Haze	★	★
Pigskin	★	★
Raw Sienna	Raw Sienna	Tumbleweed
Green Isle	Brilliant Green	Holiday Green
Spice Tan	Provincial Beige	Wicker
Midnight	Storm Blue	Indigo Blue
★	★	Light Soft Blue

❧❧❧ **Tom Cat** ❧❧❧

*This cat is a diminutive version of an early chalkware piece
(circa 1840). It's been a favorite of feline fanciers for years.
If you like cats, this one could find itself
the purrfect spot in your home.*

❧❧❧

DIRECTIONS

To prepare for this project, please read and follow the General Instructions and Basic Procedures for all projects (beginning on page 200) and the instructions for those particular Special Techniques used in this project (beginning on page 206).

Transfer and Paint the Cat

1. Transfer outline of cat to switch plate.
2. Paint background in Blue Haze.
3. Mix 4 parts Antique White and ½ part Spice Tan and use mixture to paint the body of the cat.

Transfer and Paint Cat Details

1. Transfer details of cat.
2. Mix 4 parts Spice Tan and 1 part Pigskin and use mixture to paint the cat's nose and markings.
3. Mix ½ part Jo Sonja Red and ½ part Antique White and use mixture to paint tongue and inner ears.
4. Fill in eyes with Antique White.
5. Paint irises of eyes in Blue Haze.
6. Using a stylus, dot pupils in Soft Black.
7. Paint cat's collar and the hearts in the corners of the switch plate cover in Jo Sonja Red.
8. Mix 1 part Tumbleweed and 1 part Soft Black and enough water to thin to the consistency of heavy cream and use mixture to paint the cat's whiskers. Apply with a light touch and repeat as needed. (Save this mixture to use later in project.)
9. Using mixture from step 8 above, outline the ears, eyes, mouth and one side of the nose and collar.
10. With same mixture, create a furry outline to legs.

Complete the Finishing Touches

1. Mix 1 part Tumbleweed and 1 part Soft Black and use mixture to shade cat and area behind the cat.
2. Apply antiquing mud. Allow to dry completely, at least 24 hours.
3. Using mixture from step 8 of "Transfer and Paint Cat Details," reapply whiskers if some were removed during antiquing step.
4. Finish with 2 thin coats of varnish.

55

🐦🐦 Stone House 🐦🐦

*This is my dream house—and it actually exists on a country
road very near my own 1870s farmhouse.
This stone house predates mine,
and as the three little pigs discovered,
bricks (or stones in this case) outlast the rest.*

🐦🐦

DIRECTIONS

To prepare for this project, please read and follow the General Instructions and Basic Procedures for all projects (beginning on page 200) and the instructions for those particular Special Techniques used in this project (beginning on page 206).

Paint the House
1. Draw a line to separate the roof from the house.
2. Paint house in Tumbleweed.
3. Paint roof in Soft Black.

Transfer and Paint the House Details
1. Transfer details of house to switch plate.
2. Mix 4 parts Antique White and 1 part Spice Tan and use the mixture to paint the stones.
3. Paint windows in Soft Black.
4. Paint door and chimney in Holiday Green.
5. Mix 5 parts Jo Sonja Red and ¼ part Holiday Green and use mixture to paint trim on windows, chimney, and door.
6. Paint windowsills in Holiday Green.

Complete the Finishing Touches
1. Apply antiquing mud. Allow to dry completely, at least 24 hours.
2. Finish with 2 thin coats of varnish.

Americana Heart

Red, white, and blue Stars and Stripes—a graphic statement and fun to decorate with. This one is especially fitting for the Uncle Sam and Americana devotee.

DIRECTIONS

To prepare for this project, please read and follow the General Instructions and Basic Procedures for all projects (beginning on page 200) and the instructions for those particular Special Techniques used in this project (beginning on page 206).

Paint the Field and Stripes

1. Transfer field of blue and stripes to switch plate.
2. Paint field of blue in Midnight.
3. Mix 5 parts Jo Sonja Red and ½ part Midnight and use mixture to paint red stripes.
4. Mix 5 parts Antique White and ¼ part Spice Tan and use mixture to paint white stripes. Save this mixture to use later in the project.

Transfer and Paint the Stars

1. Transfer 5 stars to switch plate cover.
2. Using mixture from step 4 of "Paint the Field and Stripes," paint the stars.

Complete the Finishing Touches

1. Apply antiquing mud. Allow to dry completely, at least 24 hours.
2. Finish with 2 thin coats of varnish.

Heart & Hand

This design was inspired by the beautiful Shaker blessing:
"Hands to work, hearts to God, blessings to be."
It would be especially appropriate
for a craft, sewing, or hobby room.

DIRECTIONS

To prepare for this project, please read and follow the General Instructions and Basic Procedures for all projects (beginning on page 200) and the instructions for those particular Special Techniques used in this project (beginning on page 206).

Transfer and Paint the Glove and Heart

1. Transfer general outline of glove, heart, and corner flowers to switch plate.
2. Paint background in Blue Haze.
3. Paint glove in Antique White.
4. Paint heart in Jo Sonja Red.
5. Mix ¼ part Tumbleweed and ¼ part Soft Black and use mixture to apply stitches in glove.
6. Using mixture from step 5 above, outline the glove.

Paint the Flowers

1. Paint centers of corner flowers in Pigskin.
2. Paint petals of flowers in Antique White.

Complete the Finishing Touches

1. Apply antiquing mud. Allow to dry completely, at least 24 hours.
2. Finish with 2 thin coats of varnish.

HISTORIC SWITCH PLATE COVERS
1	BLUE HAZE
2	ANTIQUE WHITE
3	SOFT BLACK
4	JO SONJA RED
5	PIGSKIN
6	MIDNIGHT
7	TUMBLEWEED
8	HOLIDAY GREEN

Mixtures
9	ANTIQUE WHITE + SPICE TAN
10	SPICE TAN + PIGSKIN
11	JO SONJA RED + ANTIQUE WHITE
12	TUMBLEWEED + SOFT BLACK
13	JO SONJA RED + MIDNIGHT
14	JO SONJA RED + HOLIDAY GREEN

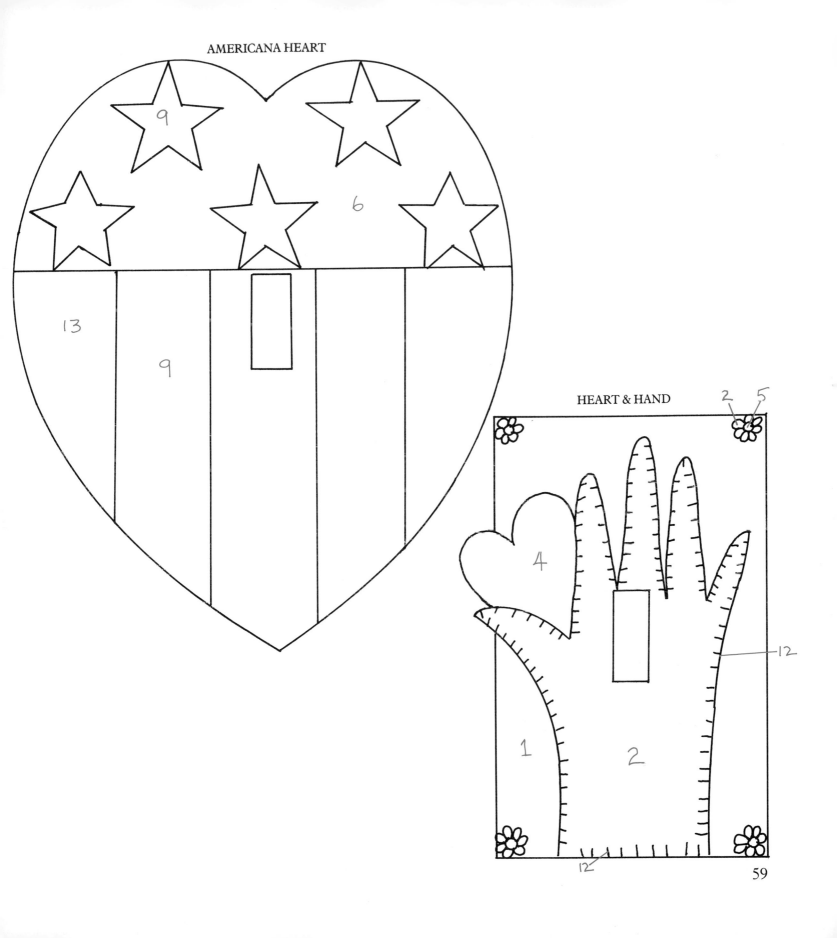

AMERICANA HEART

HEART & HAND

59

TOM CAT

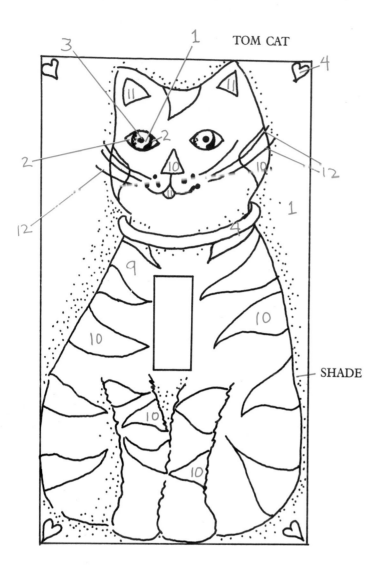

SHADE

STONE HOUSE

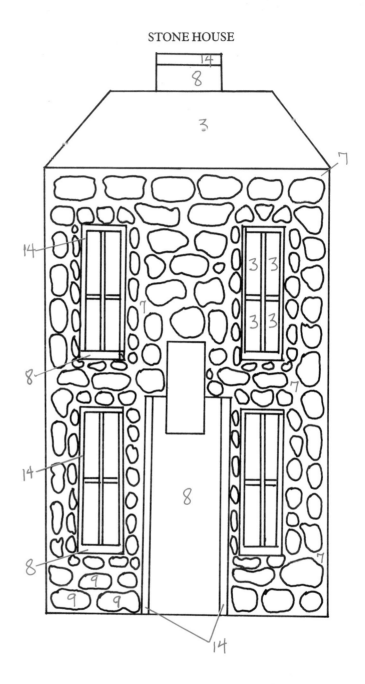

Country Whimsy

Pumpkin Harvest Carry-All

This is a quick and easy project to incorporate into your autumn decor or Halloween festivities. Fill it with Indian corn and gourds or let it overflow with dried fruits that are good for the kids and fit in with a harvest theme.

MATERIALS

Wooden pumpkin basket	Pencil *or* marking pen
Sandpaper	White transfer paper
Tack cloth	Tracing paper
Sealer	Drafting tape
Paper towels	Stylus
Acrylic palette pad	Eraser
Palette knife	Steel wool
Water containers	Varnish
1″ polyfoam sponge brush	
Brushes: #1 round; #8 flat	

PALETTE

Delta Ceramcoat	*Jo Sonja Chroma*	*Illinois Bronze*
Pumpkin	★	True Orange
Woodland Night	★	Prairie Green
Burnt Umber	★	Burnt Umber
★	★	Light Seafoam Green
Black	Carbon Black	Soft Black
Light Chocolate	★	★

DIRECTIONS

To prepare for this project, please read and follow the General Instructions and Basic Procedures for all projects (beginning on page 200) and the instructions for those particular Special Techniques used in this project (beginning on page 206).

Paint and Decorate the Basket

1. Paint entire basket, except the handle, in True Orange.
2. Paint handle in Prairie Green.
3. Transfer pattern to basket.
4. Paint stems and linework in Burnt Umber.

5. Shade pumpkin where indicated in Burnt Umber.
6. Paint leaves in Prairie Green.
7. Transfer veins and tendrils.
8. Paint veins in Soft Black.
9. Highlight veins in Light Seafoam Green.
10. Highlight leaves on one side in Light Seafoam Green.
11. Paint 1 tendril in Soft Black.
12. Paint 2 tendrils in Burnt Umber.
13. Spatter handle in True Orange.
14. Spatter basket—first in Soft Black, then in Light Seafoam Green, Burnt Umber, Prairie Green, and finally, in Light Chocolate.

PUMPKIN HARVEST CARRY-ALL
1 TRUE ORANGE
2 BURNT UMBER
4 PRAIRIE GREEN
5 SOFT BLACK
6 LIGHT SEAFOAM GREEN

Complete the Finishing Touches
1. Finish both pieces with 2 thin coats of varnish.

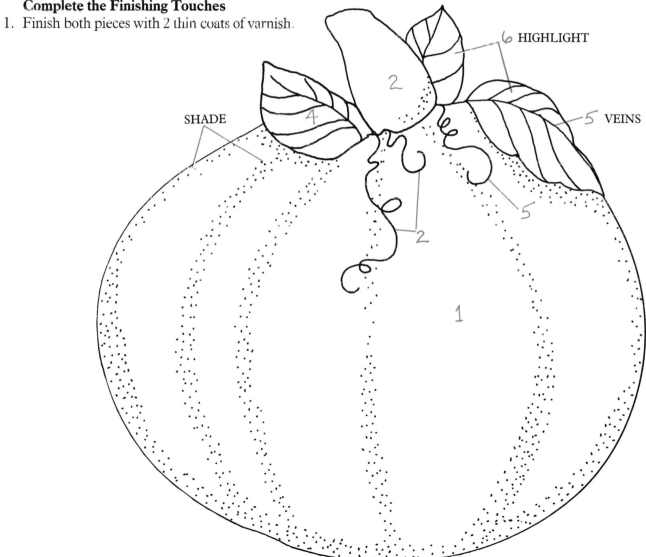

63

Clever Cat Trinket Box

I designed this trinket-sized box with cat fanciers in mind.
(Dog lovers, I've got one for you too, coming soon!)
This box works purrfectly on a small desk or nightstand
and will hold small things neatly out of sight.

MATERIALS

Wooden cat box
Sandpaper
Tack cloth
Sealer
Paper towels
Acrylic palette pad
Palette knife
Water containers
1″ polyfoam sponge brush (2)
Antiquing mud (4-oz. jar) *or* Burnt Umber oil paint
Linseed oil/mineral spirits
Brushes: #1 *or* #3 round; #8 flat

Pencil *or* marking pen
Graphite paper
Tracing paper
Drafting tape
Stylus
Eraser
Steel wool
Varnish

PALETTE

Delta Ceramcoat	*Jo Sonja Chroma*	*Illinois Bronze*
Desert Sun	★	L' Orangerie
White	Titanium White	White Wash
Straw	Yellow Oxide	Golden Harvest
Raw Sienna	Raw Sienna	Tumbleweed
Black	Carbon Black	Soft Black
Bright Red	Napthol Red Light	Jo Sonja Red
★	Colony Blue + White	Soft Blue

DIRECTIONS

To prepare for this project, please read and follow the General Instructions and Basic Procedures for all projects (beginning on page 200) and the instructions for those particular Special Techniques used in this project (beginning on page 206).

Note: Remove lid from box for ease in painting and finishing all surfaces.

Paint the Box

1. Mix 1½ parts L' Orangerie, 1½ parts White Wash, 1 part Golden Harvest, and ½ part Tumbleweed and use mixture to paint entire box.

Transfer and Paint the Cat Design

1. Transfer pattern to box. Apply paw prints randomly across the sides of the box.
2. Paint paw prints and toenails in Tumbleweed.
3. Paint markings in Tumbleweed.
4. Paint cat's irises in Soft Blue.
5. Mix ¼ part Tumbleweed and ¼ part Soft Black and use mixture to outline iris.
6. Paint pupil in Soft Black.
7. Mix ⅛ part Soft Blue and ⅛ part White Wash and use mixture to apply dots to iris.
8. Add twinkle dot in White Wash.
9. Paint heart in Soft Blue.
10. Highlight heart in White Wash.
11. Mix ¼ part Soft Blue and ¼ part Soft Black and use mixture to outline one side of the heart.
12. Mix ½ part Jo Sonja Red and ¼ part White Wash and use mixture to paint nose.
13. Shade nose in Jo Sonja Red.
14. Paint inner ear in Tumbleweed.
15. Highlight area between nose and upper lip in White Wash.
16. Using mixture from step 12 above, paint the cat's tongue.
17. Mix ½ part Soft Black and ½ part Tumbleweed and use mixture to paint whisker dots, eyelashes, and mouthline.
18. Add 1 part Tumbleweed to mixture from step 17 above and add water to thin new mixture to the consistency of whipping cream. Then, use it to paint the cat whiskers.
19. Shade cat in Tumbleweed.

Complete the Finishing Touches.

1. Apply antiquing mud. Allow to dry completely, at least 24 hours.
2. Use Outline-and-Paint technique to reapply any linework that is rubbed off during the antiquing.
3. Finish with 2 thin coats of varnish.

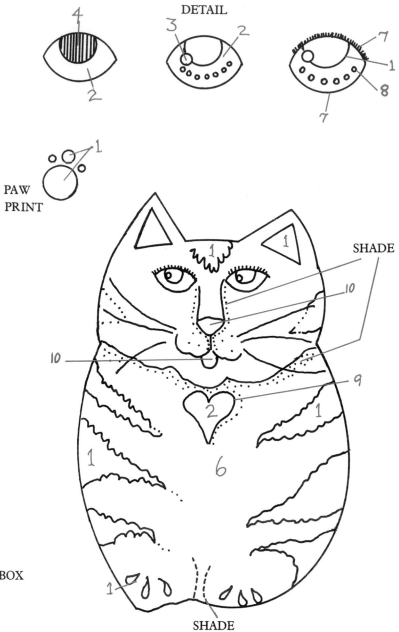

DETAIL

PAW
PRINT

SHADE

SHADE

CLEVER CAT TRINKET BOX
1 TUMBLEWEED
2 SOFT BLUE
3 WHITE WASH
4 SOFT BLACK
5 JO SONJA RED

Mixtures
6 L'ORANGERIE + WHITE WASH
   + GOLDEN HARVEST + TUMBLEWEED
7 SOFT BLACK + TUMBLEWEED
8 SOFT BLUE + WHITE WASH
9 SOFT BLUE + SOFT BLACK
10 JO SONJA RED + WHITE WASH

Autumn Sunflower Crate

*This harvest-colored crate has a double-layered design
and was brought into our shop for reproduction.
We thought it would be an excellent addition to this book
because it can hold anything from VCR tapes
to magazines to bath towels.*

MATERIALS

Wooden crate
Sandpaper
Tack cloth
Sealer
Paper towels
Acrylic palette pad
Palette knife
Water containers
1″ polyfoam sponge brush
Antiquing mud (4-oz. jar) *or* Burnt Umber oil paint
Linseed oil/mineral spirits
Wood stain (optional)
Scruffy old toothbrush *or* stencil brush
Cotton swab
Brushes: #3 *or* #5 round; ½″ stencil brush; ¾″–1½″
   glaze brush

Pencil *or* marking pen
Graphite paper
Tracing paper
Drafting tape
Stylus
Eraser
Steel wool
Varnish

PALETTE

Delta Ceramcoat	*Jo Sonja Chroma*	*Illinois Bronze*
Antique White	Warm White	Antique White
Black	Carbon Black	Soft Black
Georgia Clay	Norwegian Orange	Pennsylvania Clay
Pumpkin	⋆	True Orange
Burnt Umber	Brown Earth	Burnt Umber
Boston Fern	⋆	⋆

Country Home

VERANDA VIEWS
FROM A GEORGIA HOUSE
AMISH AUCTION IN
MONTANA MOUNTAINS
COMFORTS OF HOME
AT LOG CABIN INN
GARDENS & ANTIQUES

DIRECTIONS

To prepare for this project, please read and follow the General Instructions and Basic Procedures for all projects (beginning on page 200) and the instructions for those particular Special Techniques used in this project (beginning on page 206).

Paint and Decorate the Crate

1. Paint one end of the crate in Antique White. If you plan to paint sunflowers on both ends, then paint both ends in Antique White.
2. Transfer pattern A onto painted end of crate.
3. Paint stems in Burnt Umber.
4. Paint leaves in Boston Fern.
5. Using Transparent Wash technique, paint a wash of Boston Fern over the stems.
6. Mix 2 parts Boston Fern and ½ part Antique White and use mixture to highlight left leaf.
7. Mix 1 part True Orange, 1 part Antique White and ½ part Boston Fern and use mixture to highlight middle stem.
8. Using ½″ stencil brush, fill in all flower centers in Burnt Umber.
9. Paint petals in Pennsylvania Clay.
10. Align and transfer pattern B directly over painted pattern A.
11. Paint these petals in True Orange.
12. Paint the small petals that originate from the center of the flowers in Burnt Umber.
13. Using ½″ stencil brush, fill in the flower centers again in Burnt Umber.
14. Dampen all the Burnt Umber flower centers and using stencil brush, highlight inner areas in True Orange, using a light touch.
15. Shade crate behind all petals and stems with Burnt Umber.
16. Repeat steps 2–15 if you are painting both ends of crate.

Complete the Finishing Touches

1. Apply antiquing mud. Allow to dry completely, at least 24 hours. (Use cotton swab to remove mud on each petal.)
2. Using commercial stain *or* a mixture of 2 tablespoons antiquing mud, 2 tablespoons mineral spirits, and ⅛ teaspoon linseed oil, stain remaining areas of crate.
3. Mix 2 parts Black and 2 parts Burnt Umber and use mixture and the Spattering technique to spatter crate, mostly in the background areas.
4. Finish with 2 thin coats of varnish.

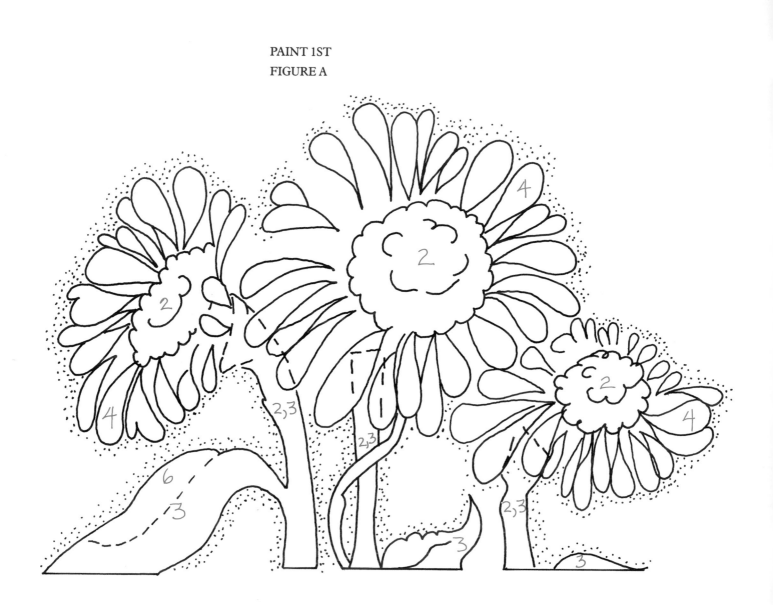

AUTUMN SUNFLOWER CRATE
1   ANTIQUE WHITE
2   BURNT UMBER
3   BOSTON FERN
4   PENNSYLVANIA CLAY
5   TRUE ORANGE

Mixtures
6   BOSTON FERN + ANTIQUE WHITE
7   TRUE ORANGE + ANTIQUE WHITE + BOSTON FERN

PAINT 2ND
FIGURE B

ALL PETALS ARE TRUE ORANGE

Moon-Man Gameboard

Gameboards are a favorite of mine. I enjoy seeing a group of them on a wall; they add a sense of whimsy, charm, and interest to a room. In the early days of our country, craftsmen who made them usually painted one side in the traditional checkerboard pattern and the other side in the pattern for pachisi. After you paint this piece, consider it a family heirloom and pass it from one generation to the next.

MATERIALS

Wooden checkerboard and shaped checkers
Sandpaper
Tack cloth
Sealer
Paper towels
Acrylic palette pad
Palette knife
Water containers
1½″ polyfoam sponge brushes (2)
Antiquing mud (4-oz. jar) *or* Burnt Umber oil paint
    and .34 oz. tube of Prussian Blue oil paint
Linseed oil/mineral spirits
Muslin bag to store checkers (optional)
Brushes: #10 *or* #12 flat; #3 *or* #5 round; ⅝″ stencil brush

Pencil *or* marking pen
Graphite paper
Tracing paper
Drafting tape
Stylus
Eraser
Ruler
Steel wool
Varnish

PALETTE

Delta Ceramcoat	*Jo Sonja Chroma*	*Illinois Bronze*
Pale Yellow	Cadmium Yellow Light + White	Light Cactus Flower
★	★	Light Pink Blossom
Dark Night	Storm Blue	Liberty Blue
★	Colony Blue + White	Soft Blue
★	★	Apache Red
Empire Gold	Turner's Yellow	Dijon Gold
Burnt Sienna	Burnt Sienna	Burnt Sienna
Cadet Gray	Nimbus Grey	Soft Grey

DIRECTIONS

To prepare for this project, please read and follow the General Instructions and Basic Procedures for all projects (beginning on page 200) and the instructions for those particular Special Techniques used in this project (beginning on page 206).

Transfer and Paint the Moon-Man

1. Paint entire board in Liberty Blue.
2. Transfer the general outline of the moon-man onto one end of the board, and then flip the paper over and transfer the moon-man onto the other end of the board.

3. Mix 4 parts of Light Cactus Flower with 4 parts of Light Pink Blossom and use the mixture to paint the faces. You may need to apply 3 or 4 coats.
4. Shade the general outlines of the faces in Liberty Blue.
5. Transfer the facial details onto the faces.
6. Using the Dry Brush technique, apply Apache Red to the cheek areas.
7. Paint the iris of each eye in Soft Blue.
8. Paint the pupils in Liberty Blue.
9. Paint twinkle dot of eye in mixture from step 3 above.

10. Shade around the eyes and eyelids in Liberty Blue.
11. Paint the hats in Dijon Gold. You may need to apply 3 or 4 coats.
12. Paint the lips in Apache Red.
13. Outline the lips in Burnt Sienna.
14. Shade under the lower lips in Burnt Sienna.
15. Paint the eyebrows in 1 coat of Soft Grey.
16. Paint 1 coat of Burnt Sienna on top of the Soft Grey on the eyebrows.
17. Using Soft Grey, shade a second coat under the nostrils, under the lips, under the brows, around the eyelids, on the chins, and next to the hats.
18. Shade hat in Burnt Sienna.
19. Paint the eyelash lines and lower lid in Liberty Blue.
20. Outline the right side of each iris in Liberty Blue.

Transfer and Paint the Checkerboard
1. Transfer the checkerboard area.
2. Paint alternate squares in Soft Blue. You may need to apply 3 or 4 coats.

Paint the Game Pieces
1. Paint the moon-shaped game pieces in Dijon Gold.
2. Using mixture from step 3 of "Transfer and Paint the Moon-Man," paint the star-shaped game pieces.

Complete the Finishing Touches
1. Distress gameboard, if desired.
2. Sand the gameboard to age it.
3. Mix 1 part Prussian Blue oil paint to 4 parts antiquing mud and use mixture to antique the gameboard and the game pieces.
4. Finish with 3 or 4 thin coats of varnish.

REPEAT CHECKERBOARD PATTERN FOR A TOTAL OF 8 ROWS OF 8 SQUARES.

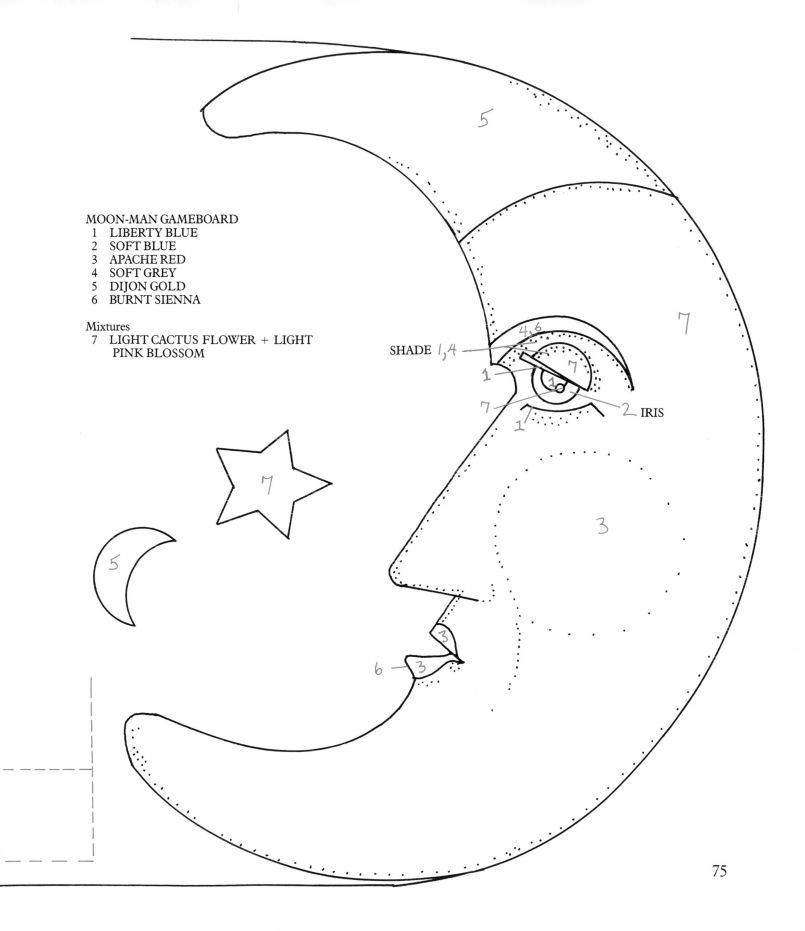

MOON-MAN GAMEBOARD
1   LIBERTY BLUE
2   SOFT BLUE
3   APACHE RED
4   SOFT GREY
5   DIJON GOLD
6   BURNT SIENNA

Mixtures
7   LIGHT CACTUS FLOWER + LIGHT
    PINK BLOSSOM

SHADE 1,4

IRIS

75

Folk Guardian Angel

*Angels have always been a favorite of mine. Currently,
they seem to be soaring in popularity, causing me
to ponder anew the theory that they are celestial guardians
who mingle with and protect us. I find these stories
charming and warming to the human spirit. I hope they
are true, and that those guardian angels approve of
our efforts—yours and mine.*

MATERIALS

Wooden angel
Sandpaper
Tack cloth
Sealer
Paper towels
Acrylic palette pad
Palette knife
Water containers
1″ polyfoam sponge brush
Linseed oil/mineral spirits
Antiquing mud (4-oz. jar) *or* Burnt Umber oil paint
Brushes: #2 *or* #4 flat; #6 *or* #8 flat; #1 script liner;
   #1 round; #2 *or* #3 round

Pencil *or* marking pen
White transfer paper
Tracing paper
Drafting tape
Stylus
Eraser
Cotton swabs
Steel wool
Varnish

PALETTE

Delta Ceramcoat	*Jo Sonja Chroma*	*Illinois Bronze*
Dusty Mauve	★	★
Ivory	Titanium White	White Wash
Empire Gold	Turner's Yellow	Dijon Gold
Burnt Sienna	Burnt Sienna	Burnt Sienna
Midnight	Storm Blue	Indigo Blue
Black	Carbon Black	Soft Black
★	★	Jo Sonja Red
Forest Green	Green Oxide	Green Olive
Dresden Flesh	★	★

DIRECTIONS

To prepare for this project, please read and follow the General Instructions and Basic Procedures for all projects (beginning on page 200) and the instructions for those particular Special Techniques used in this project (beginning on page 206).

Transfer and Paint the Angel and Gown

1. Transfer general outlines of gown, sleeves, face, neck, wing, halo, and hair.
2. Mix 4 parts Midnight and ¼ part Soft Black and use mixture to paint gown.
3. Paint sleeves, halo, and shoes in Dusty Mauve.
4. Mix 2¼ parts Jo Sonja Red and ¼ part Midnight and use mixture to shade halo, sleeve, and shoes.
5. Paint bands on gown and sleeve in White Wash.
6. Mix 4 parts Dresden Flesh and 1 part Dijon Gold and use mixture to paint wing.
7. Paint flesh in Dresden Flesh.
8. Shade flesh in Burnt Sienna.
9. Paint hair in Burnt Sienna.
10. Mix ½ part Burnt Sienna and ½ part Soft Black and use mixture to add wispy lines to damp (not wet) hair.

Transfer and Paint the Facial Features

1. Transfer remaining elements of pattern.
2. Paint eyebrows and outline chin line in Burnt Sienna.
3. Shade under eyebrows and under chin line in Burnt Sienna.
4. Mix ¼ part Dresden Flesh and ¼ part Burnt Sienna and use mixture to outline nose and mouth.
5. Mix ¼ part Jo Sonja Red and ¼ part Dusty Mauve and use mixture to paint mouth.
6. Dampen lower lip and highlight with a touch of Dresden Flesh.
7. Outline mouth again in Jo Sonja Red.
8. Mix ¼ part Soft Black, ¼ part Midnight, and ¼ part Burnt Sienna and use mixture to paint eyelashes. Paint thin, wispy lines.
9. Using mixture from step 4 above, apply eye shadow. Let dry.
10. Mix ¼ part White Wash and ¼ part Midnight and use mixture and Side-Loaded Color technique to apply directly over the eye shadow.
11. Using mixture from step 4 above and Side-Loaded Color technique, paint a dimple in the angel's chin.
12. Mix ½ part Jo Sonja Red and ½ part Dresden Flesh and use mixture and Floated Color technique with a light touch to paint cheeks. Repeat as needed to obtain depth of color desired.

Transfer and Paint the Leaves

1. Transfer leaves, linework, and stems.
2. Paint leaves on bands at the bottom of the gown in Forest Green.
3. Paint most of the large leaves on the gown in Forest Green. (Refer to photo.)
4. Mix ½ part Forest Green and ½ part White Wash and use mixture to paint remaining leaves. Save this mixture to use later in the project.
5. Using Double-Loaded Color technique, paint wing leaves in Forest Green and Black.
6. Mix 1½ parts Forest Green, 1 part White Wash, ¹⁄₁₀ part Dijon Gold and enough water to thin mixture to a heavy cream consistency and use mixture to paint stems.

Transfer and Paint the Flowers

1. Transfer general outline of flowers.
2. Paint circles of filler flowers on top of the White Wash band in Dusty Mauve.
3. Add Dijon Gold dot to center of circles.
4. Transfer petals.
5. Mix 2 parts White Wash and 2 parts Midnight. Load brush in mixture and side-load in Midnight using Double-Loaded Color technique. Apply with the Midnight side of the brush toward center dot of the flower.
6. Repaint center dots in Dijon Gold.
7. Paint balls for folk roses on gown and wing in Dusty Mauve.
8. Transfer details of roses.
9. Mix 2¼ parts Jo Sonja Red and ¼ part Midnight and use mixture to shade roses.
10. Using Side-Loaded Color technique, paint the 1 petal emanating from shaded areas of roses in White Wash.
11. Using mixture from step 9 above and Comma Strokes, add detail petals to each rose.
12. Paint stamens in Dijon Gold.
13. Using mixture from step 4 of "Transfer and Paint the Leaves," paint small ball at base of each rose.
14. Using the same mixture, add linework on top of wing.

Complete the Finishing Touches

1. Paint scallops on wing in Dusty Mauve.
2. Apply antiquing mud. Allow to dry completely, at least 24 hours. Some people prefer not to antique the face, but if you do antique it, just a hint of color is all that is needed.
3. Finish with 2 or 3 thin coats of varnish.

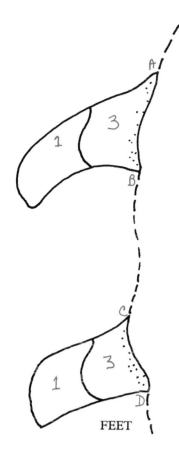

FOLK GUARDIAN ANGEL
1 DUSTY MAUVE
2 WHITE WASH
3 DRESDEN FLESH
4 BURNT SIENNA
5 JO SONJA RED
6 FOREST GREEN
7 SOFT BLACK
8 DIJON GOLD

Mixtures
9   BURNT SIENNA + SOFT BLACK
10 DRESDEN FLESH + BURNT SIENNA
11 JO SONJA RED + DUSTY MAUVE
12 SOFT BLACK + MIDNIGHT + BURNT SIENNA
13 WHITE WASH + MIDNIGHT
14 JO SONJA RED + DRESDEN FLESH
15 FOREST GREEN + WHITE WASH
16 JO SONJA RED + MIDNIGHT
17 DRESDEN FLESH + DIJON GOLD
18 FOREST GREEN + WHITE WASH + DIJON GOLD
19 MIDNIGHT + SOFT BLACK

FEET

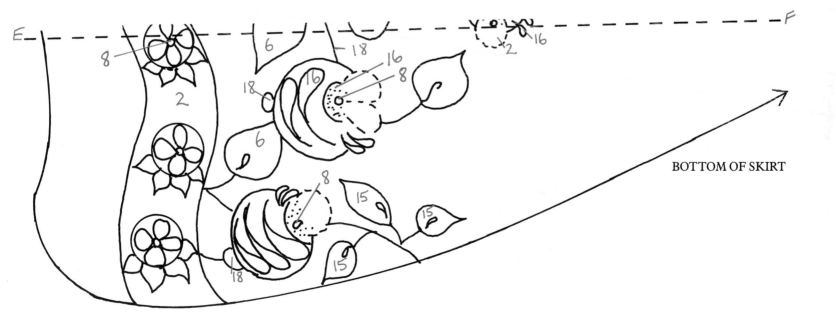

BOTTOM OF SKIRT

79

WING

80

81

Moon-Man Jewelry Box

This celestial box will hold all kinds of small but important treasures. My husband's is on his desk at work; he tells me it's a wonderful conversation piece.

MATERIALS

Wooden crescent box
Sandpaper
Tack cloth
Sealer
Paper towels
Acrylic palette pad
Palette knife
Antiquing mud (4-oz. jar) *or* Burnt Umber oil paint
Linseed oil/mineral spirits
Brushes: #10 *or* #12 flat; #3 *or* #5 round; ⅝"
    stencil brush

Pencil *or* marking pen
Water containers
1" polyfoam sponge brush
Graphite paper
Tracing paper
Drafting tape
Stylus
Eraser
Steel wool
Varnish

PALETTE

Delta Ceramcoat	*Jo Sonja Chroma*	*Illinois Bronze*
Dark Night	Storm Blue	Liberty Blue
Pale Yellow	Cadmium Yellow Light + White	Light Cactus Flower
★	★	Light Pink Blossom
★	★	Apache Red
★	Colony Blue + White	Soft Blue
Burnt Sienna	Burnt Sienna	Burnt Sienna
Cadet Gray	Nimbus Grey	Soft Grey
Empire Gold	Turner's Yellow	Dijon Gold
Burnt Umber	Brown Earth	Burnt Umber

DIRECTIONS

To prepare for this project, please read and follow the General Instructions and Basic Procedures for all projects (beginning on page 200) and the instructions for those particular Special Techniques used in this project (beginning on page 206).

Note: You may want to remove the lid for ease in painting and finishing.

Transfer and Paint the Face and Hat

1. Transfer line separating hat from face onto lid.
2. Paint the hat on the lid and all the surfaces of the box in Liberty Blue.

3. Mix 3 parts Light Cactus Flower with 3 parts Light Pink Blossom and use mixture to paint the face. You may need to apply 3 coats. (Save this mixture to use later in the project.)
4. Transfer facial features.
5. Shade face in Liberty Blue.
6. Using Dry Brush Color technique, apply Apache Red to cheek area.
7. Paint iris of eye in Soft Blue.
8. Paint pupil in Liberty Blue.
9. Shade around eye and eyelid in Liberty Blue.
10. Mix 1 part Apache Red with ¼ part Burnt Sienna and use mixture to paint lips.
11. Outline lips, eyelid, and nostril in Burnt Sienna.

12. Paint eyebrow in 1 coat of Soft Grey.
13. Paint 1 coat of Burnt Sienna over Soft Grey eyebrow.
14. Using Soft Grey, shade under the nostril, under the lip, around the eyelid, on the chin, and next to the hat.
15. Paint eye line and lower lid line in Liberty Blue.
16. Outline left side of iris in Liberty Blue.
17. Using Soft Blue, highlight one side of hat.

Add the Stars and Decorate
1. Transfer small stars onto sides of box in a random manner.

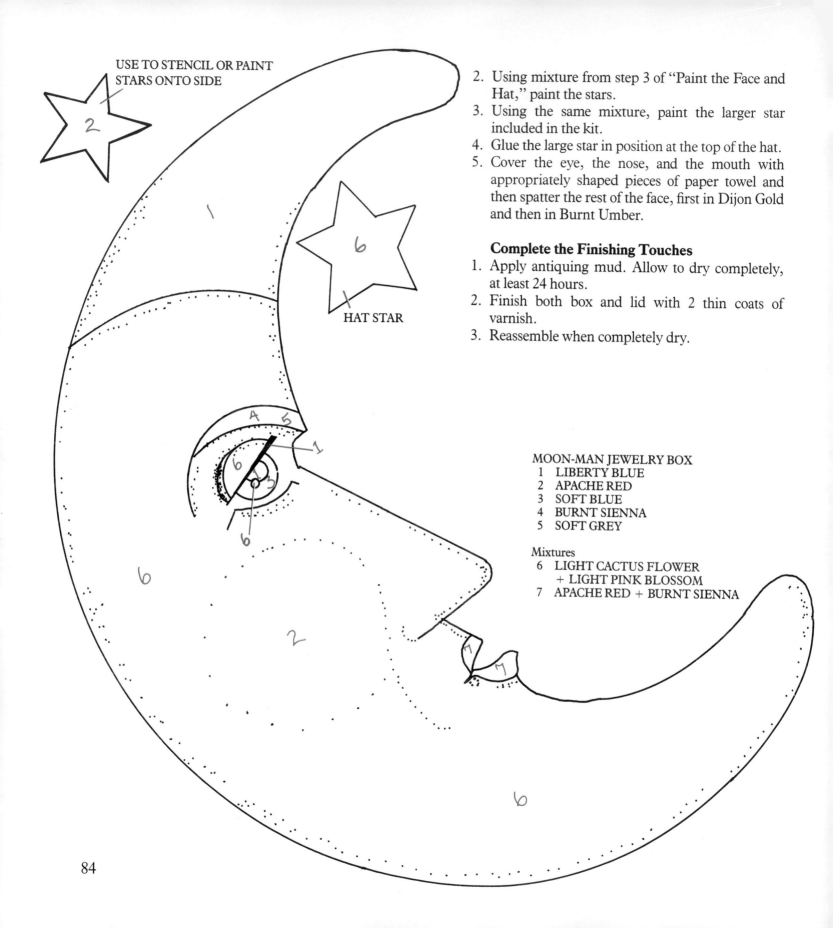

USE TO STENCIL OR PAINT
STARS ONTO SIDE

2

1

6

HAT STAR

2. Using mixture from step 3 of "Paint the Face and Hat," paint the stars.
3. Using the same mixture, paint the larger star included in the kit.
4. Glue the large star in position at the top of the hat.
5. Cover the eye, the nose, and the mouth with appropriately shaped pieces of paper towel and then spatter the rest of the face, first in Dijon Gold and then in Burnt Umber.

Complete the Finishing Touches
1. Apply antiquing mud. Allow to dry completely, at least 24 hours.
2. Finish both box and lid with 2 thin coats of varnish.
3. Reassemble when completely dry.

MOON-MAN JEWELRY BOX
1 LIBERTY BLUE
2 APACHE RED
3 SOFT BLUE
4 BURNT SIENNA
5 SOFT GREY

Mixtures
6 LIGHT CACTUS FLOWER
   + LIGHT PINK BLOSSOM
7 APACHE RED + BURNT SIENNA

Angel Keepsake Box

*Although this box was designed to hold jewelry,
we keep ours in the living room to hold playing cards.
I know a woman who has an angel collection and uses
this box to hold her "mini-angels." She keeps the lid
standing up behind it, which looks very charming.
Shown, page 83.*

MATERIALS

Wooden jewelry box
Sandpaper
Tack cloth
Sealer
Paper towels
Acrylic palette pad
Palette knife
Water containers
1″ polyfoam sponge brush
Scruffy old toothbrush
Brushes: #1 *or* #3 round; #8 flat

Pencil *or* marking pen
Graphite paper
Tracing paper
Drafting tape
Stylus
Eraser
Steel wool
Varnish

PALETTE

Delta Ceramcoat	*Jo Sonja Chroma*	*Illinois Bronze*
Medium Flesh	Opal	Light Peaches n' Cream
Pigskin	★	★
Boston Fern	★	★
Bright Red	Napthol Red Light	Jo Sonja Red
White	Titanium White	White Wash
Raw Sienna	Raw Sienna	Tumbleweed
Black	Carbon Black	Soft Black

DIRECTIONS

To prepare for this project, please read and follow the General Instructions and Basic Procedures for all projects (beginning on page 200) and the instructions for those particular Special Techniques used in this project (beginning on page 206).

Transfer the Angel Pattern and Paint the Angel and Box

1. Transfer the general angel pattern onto box.
2. Paint angel face, neck, and arms in Light Peaches n' Cream.
3. Shade face, neck, and arms with Tumbleweed.
4. Outline face and neck in Tumbleweed.
5. Paint angel gown in Pigskin.
6. Shade gown in Boston Fern.
7. Mix 10 parts Jo Sonja Red and 1⅛ parts Boston Fern and use mixture to paint hearts. (Refer to photo.) Save this mixture to use later in the project.
8. Paint background and remaining areas of box (except legs) in Boston Fern.
9. Paint inside of box in your choice of color. (I painted mine in Boston Fern.)
10. Paint legs of box in Pigskin.
11. Using mixture from step 7 above, outline legs of box.
12. Paint the 2 pairs of wings in White Wash.
13. Shade wings in Pigskin.
14. Using Pigskin, add petal strokes to bottom corners of lid.

Transfer and Paint Angel Details

1. Paint angel hair and eyebrows in Tumbleweed.
2. Mix 1 part White Wash and 2 parts Tumbleweed and use mixture to highlight hair. Apply strokes with a light touch.
3. Transfer details.
4. Shade behind eyes in Boston Fern.
5. Paint white of each eye in White Wash.
6. Transfer eye detail.
7. Paint iris of each eye in Tumbleweed.
8. Outline each iris in Boston Fern.
9. Paint pupils in Soft Black.
10. Outline upper and lower eyelids in Tumbleweed.
11. Paint eyelash lines in Boston Fern.
12. Paint nose line in Tumbleweed.
13. Using Floated Color technique, paint cheeks in Jo Sonja Red.
14. Paint mouth outline in Tumbleweed.
15. Using mixture from step 7 of "Paint the Angel and Box," fill in mouth.
16. Using Jo Sonja Red, fill in mouth again, over the mixed paint.
17. Dampen face with clear water and apply a hint of Jo Sonja Red to chin, nose, and forehead, using Side-Loaded Color technique. A hint of color is all that is needed.

Complete the Finishing Touches

1. Use sandpaper to age the legs, corners, and edges of box.
2. Cover angel's face and hair with appropriately sized pieces of paper towel and apply spattering, first in Pigskin, then in White Wash, and finally, in Soft Black.
3. Finish with 2 thin coats of varnish.

ANGEL KEEPSAKE BOX
1 LIGHT PEACHES N' CREAM
2 TUMBLEWEED
3 PIGSKIN
4 BOSTON FERN
5 WHITE WASH
6 SOFT BLACK
7 JO SONJA RED

Mixtures
8 JO SONJA RED + BOSTON FERN
9 WHITE WASH + TUMBLEWEED

LEFT CORNER

RIGHT CORNER

87

Kittens and Bows Doorstop

I have doors in my home that just don't want to stay open on their own; they need a little help. A brick would do the job but would lack detail and interest (and is awfully hard on bare toes). This piece is the cat's meow as a sturdy doorstop and has a tapered base to wedge under the door.

MATERIALS
Wooden cat doorstop kit
Sandpaper
Tack cloth
Sealer
Paper towels
Acrylic palette pad
Palette knife
Water containers
Small piece of natural sponge
Scruffy old toothbrush *or* cotton swab
1″ polyfoam sponge brush (2)
Antiquing mud (4-oz. jar) *or* Burnt Umber oil paint
Linseed oil/mineral spirits
Brushes: #8 flat; #1 round; ¾″–1½″ glaze brush

Pencil *or* marking pen
White transfer paper
Tracing paper
Drafting tape
Stylus
Eraser
Steel wool
Varnish
Wood glue *or* glue gun
Screwdriver
Fabric or paper ribbon

PALETTE

Delta Ceramcoat	*Jo Sonja Chroma*	*Illinois Bronze*
Raw Sienna	Raw Sienna	Tumbleweed
Bright Red	Napthol Red Light	Jo Sonja Red
White	Titanium White	White Wash
Woodland Night	★	Prairie Green
Black	Carbon Black	Soft Black
Queen Anne's Lace	Warm White + Norwegian Orange	Light Blonde
★	★	Light Seafoam Green

DIRECTIONS

To prepare for this project, please read and follow the General Instructions and Basic Procedures for all projects (beginning on page 200) and the instructions for those particular Special Techniques used in this project (beginning on page 206).

Note: Omit finishing for 3″–4″ on each end of the handle since you will glue the handle into the slots on the back of the basket when painting is completed.

Paint the Basket and Base

1. Basecoat the leafy area behind the cats, the handle, the grooved basket and all edges in 1 coat of Tumbleweed.
2. Using Transparent Wash technique, apply Prairie Green to basket. Repeat as needed for desired depth of color.
3. Paint top side of base (the horizontal area "beneath" the basket) in 1 coat of Prairie Green.
4. Paint edge of base in 1 coat of White Wash. (This will form the white checks later.)
5. Paint alternate checks on front of the base in Soft Black.

Paint the Cats and Bows

1. Paint cats in Light Blonde.
2. Shade cats in Tumbleweed.
3. Paint bows in Jo Sonja Red.
4. Shade bows in Prairie Green.

Transfer and Paint Leaf and Flower Designs

1. Transfer leaf design (except veins). Extend leaf design slightly into area directly behind the cats.
2. Paint all the leaves with veins in Prairie Green.
3. Paint the unveined leaves in Soft Black.
4. Transfer the leaf veins.
5. Paint all veins in Light Seafoam Green.
6. Transfer the roses.
7. Paint the roses in Jo Sonja Red.
8. Shade the roses in Prairie Green.
9. Add center dots to the roses in Light Blonde.

Transfer and Paint Cat Details

1. Transfer the details of the cats.
2. Mix 1 part Jo Sonja Red and 1 part Light Blonde and use mixture to paint inner ears and noses of the cats.
3. Shade bottom of noses and 1 side of each ear in Tumbleweed.
4. Mix ½ part Tumbleweed and ⅛ part Soft Black and use mixture to paint the cats' mouths.
5. Paint whiskers and eyelids in Tumbleweed.
6. Paint the irises of the eyes in Prairie Green.
7. Add tiny dots to the bottom halves of the irises in Light Seafoam Green.
8. Add pupils to eyes in Soft Black.
9. Add twinkle dots to eyes in White Wash.
10. Outline around irises in Soft Black.

Complete the Finishing Touches

1. Using a natural sponge and the Sponge Painting technique, add Light Seafoam Green to the base.
2. Test-fit the handle into the slots on the back of the basket. Keep the handle ½″ up from the bottom of the slot to avoid marring it. The fit should be snug.
3. Paint narrow stripes across the grain of the handle, alternating with Soft Black, White Wash, and Prairie Green.
4. Apply a small amount of glue into each slot and insert the handle. (Caution people not to pick up the basket by the handle—the handle is strictly decorative and is not intended to be functional.)
5. Glue and screw the base onto the basket. Use glue sparingly; you don't want excess glue to ooze out and mar your work.
6. Glue the cats and their bows in the appropriate positions.
7. Apply antiquing mud. Allow to dry completely, at least 24 hours. (Use a cotton swab or scruffy brush to fill in the grooves in the basket.)
8. Reapply any linework, such as whiskers, that may have been rubbed off while antiquing.
9. Finish with 2 coats of varnish.
10. Attach ribbon bow if desired.

KITTENS AND BOWS DOORSTOP
1 TUMBLEWEED
2 PRAIRIE GREEN
3 LIGHT BLONDE
4 JO SONJA RED
5 SOFT BLACK
6 LIGHT SEAFOAM GREEN
7 WHITE WASH

Mixtures
8 JO SONJA RED + LIGHT BLONDE
9 TUMBLEWEED + SOFT BLACK

6 ALL VEINS

SHADE

SHADE

SHADE

91

Country
Kitchen

Apple-Lemon Heart Clock

I love hearts used in any decorative manner—on jewelry, shelves, pictures, and this clock. The heart shape is appealing and lends itself to folk art embellishments like the mix of red apples and yellow lemons which make this piece fun and happy and perfect for the heart of the home.

MATERIALS

Wooden heart clock
Sandpaper
Tack cloth
Sealer
Paper towels
Acrylic palette pad
Palette knife
Water containers
1″ polyfoam sponge brush
Antiquing mud (4-oz. jar) *or* Burnt Umber oil paint
Linseed oil/mineral spirits
Brushes: #8, #10, or #12 flat

Pencil *or* marking pen
Graphite paper
Tracing paper
Drafting tape
Stylus
Eraser
Steel wool
Varnish
Spray adhesive

PALETTE

Delta Ceramcoat	*Jo Sonja Chroma*	*Illinois Bronze*
★	★	Light Stoneware Blue
Bright Red	Napthol Red Light	Jo Sonja Red
Woodland Night	★	Prairie Green
Empire Gold	Turner's Yellow	Dijon Gold
Black	Carbon Black	Soft Black
Pumpkin	★	True Orange
Mendocino	Burgundy	Bordeaux

DIRECTIONS

To prepare for this project, please read and follow the General Instructions and Basic Procedures for all projects (beginning on page 200) and the instructions for those particular Special Techniques used in this project (beginning on page 206).

Paint and Decorate the Clock

1. Paint face and sides of clock in Light Stoneware Blue. Do not paint the 4″ circle in the center. (The dial face included in your kit will be glued there.)
2. Transfer the fruits and leaves pattern.
3. Paint leaves in Prairie Green.
4. Paint lemons in Dijon Gold.
5. Paint apples in Jo Sonja Red.
6. Paint veins in leaves, stem and blossom end of apples in Soft Black.
7. Transfer striping around design area following contour of heart.
8. Paint striping in Jo Sonja Red.
9. Paint outer edge in Jo Sonja Red.
10. Shade lemons in True Orange.
11. Shade apples in Bordeaux.

Complete the Finishing Touches

1. Apply antiquing mud. Allow to dry completely, at least 24 hours.
2. Highlight one side of each apple in True Orange.
3. Finish with 2 or 3 thin coats of varnish.
4. Install dial face and clock mechanism following kit instructions.

APPLE-LEMON HEART CLOCK
1 LIGHT STONEWARE BLUE
2 DIJON GOLD
3 JO SONJA RED
4 SOFT BLACK
5 PRAIRIE GREEN
6 TRUE ORANGE
7 BORDEAUX

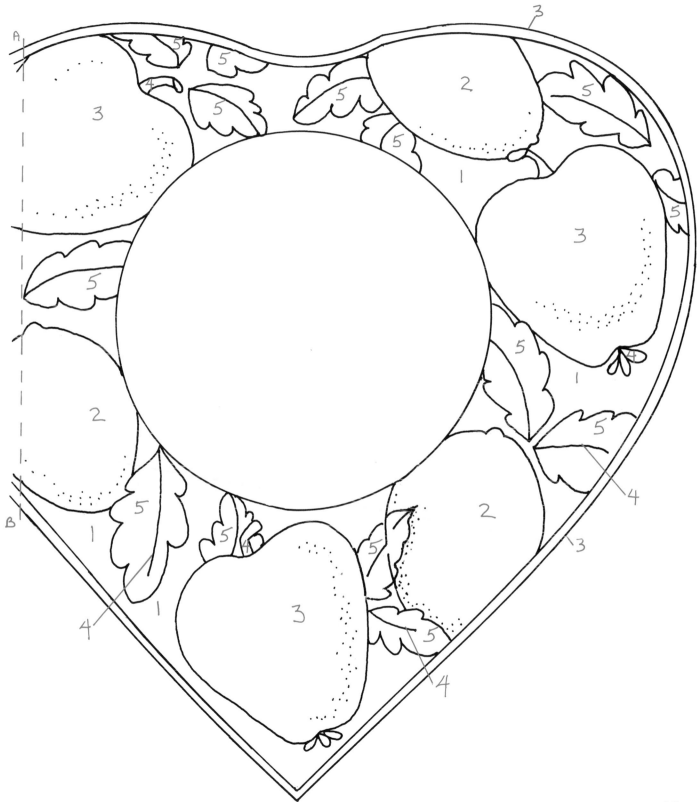

Apple-Citrus Heart Footstool

Children love this stool, and we know one little girl who carries it around the house with her. Even if she sits on the couch, the stool sits with her! It also makes a nice step stool for the bathroom so little ones can brush their teeth. Shown, page 92.

MATERIALS

Wooden heart footstool
Sandpaper
Tack cloth
Sealer
Paper towels
Acrylic palette pad
Palette knife
Water containers
1½″ polyfoam sponge brush
Antiquing mud (4-oz. jar) *or* Burnt Umber oil paint
Linseed oil/mineral spirits
Brushes: #1 round; #8 flat

Pencil *or* marking pen
Graphite paper
Tracing paper
Drafting tape
Stylus
Eraser
Steel wool
Varnish

PALETTE

Delta Ceramcoat	*Jo Sonja Chroma*	*Illinois Bronze*
Mendocino	Burgundy	Bordeaux
Bright Red	Napthol Red Light	Jo Sonja Red
Pumpkin	★	True Orange
Empire Gold	Turner's Yellow	Dijon Gold
Woodland Night	★	Prairie Green
Black	Carbon Black	Soft Black
Cape Code + White	French Blue + Titanium White	Light Stoneware Blue
Burnt Umber	Brown Earth	Burnt Umber

DIRECTIONS

To prepare for this project, please read and follow the General Instructions and Basic Procedures for all projects (beginning on page 200) and the instructions for those particular Special Techniques used in this project (beginning on page 206).

APPLE-CITRUS HEART FOOTSTOOL
1 JO SONJA RED
2 DIJON GOLD
3 TRUE ORANGE
4 LIGHT STONEWARE BLUE
5 SOFT BLACK
6 BURNT UMBER
7 PRAIRIE GREEN
8 BORDEAUX

EXTEND OVER SIDE OF STOOL

Paint and Decorate the Stool

1. Paint stool in Light Stoneware Blue.
2. Transfer pattern to stool.
3. Paint lemons in Dijon Gold.
4. Paint oranges in True Orange.
5. Paint apples in Jo Sonja Red.
6. Paint all stems in Burnt Umber.
7. Paint lined leaves in Soft Black.
8. Paint large leaves with veins in Prairie Green.
9. Transfer veins onto large leaves.
10. Paint veins in Soft Black.
11. Paint stripes on legs in Jo Sonja Red. (Refer to photo.)
12. Shade lemons in True Orange.
13. Shade apples and oranges in Bordeaux.

Complete the Finishing Touches

1. Apply antiquing mud. Allow to dry completely, at least 24 hours.
2. Finish with 2 or 3 thin coats of varnish.

97

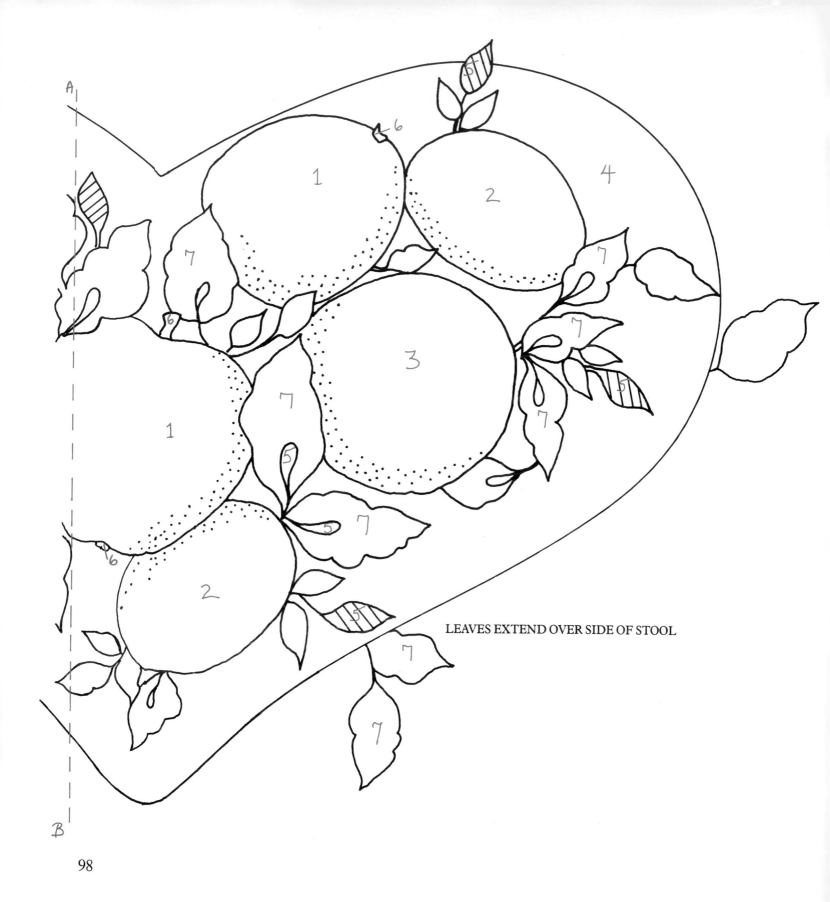

LEAVES EXTEND OVER SIDE OF STOOL

Tall Victorian House Box

You can fill this multipurpose container with spaghetti and use as a canister, along with its smaller kitchen companions—the recipe box and cottage. Or, you can fill it with sand and use it as a doorstop.

MATERIALS

Wooden house box
Sandpaper
Tack cloth
Sealer
Paper towels
Acrylic palette pad
Palette knife
Water containers
Antiquing mud (4-oz. jar) *or* Burnt Umber oil paint
1″ polyfoam sponge brush
Brushes: #8 flat; ¼″ stencil brush

Pencil *or* marking pen
Graphite paper
Tracing paper
Drafting tape
Stylus
Eraser
Ruler
Wood glue *or* glue gun
Steel wool
Varnish

PALETTE

Delta Ceramcoat	*Jo Sonja Chroma*	*Illinois Bronze*
Woodland Night	★	Prairie Green
Bright Red	Napthol Red Light	Jo Sonja Red
White	Titanium White	White Wash
Black Green	★	Prairie Green + Soft Black
Light Chocolate	Provincial Beige	Wicker
Burnt Umber	Brown Earth	Burnt Umber
★	★	Light Seafoam Green
Black	Carbon Black	Soft Black

DIRECTIONS

To prepare for this project, please read and follow the General Instructions and Basic Procedures for all projects (beginning on page 200) and the instructions for those particular Special Techniques used in this project (beginning on page 206).

Paint the House

1. Draw a horizontal line 1½″ up from the bottom all around the house.
2. Mix 5 parts Jo Sonja Red and ¼ part Prairie Green and use the mixture to paint the bottom 1½″ area. (Save this mixture to use later in the project.)

3. Draw a line 1″ up from the red band all around the house.
4. Paint this 1″ area and the chimney in Prairie Green.
5. Paint the rest of the house in Light Chocolate.
6. Transfer bricks onto the house.
7. Paint bricks on the house in Burnt Umber very faintly, using Dry Brush Color technique.
8. Using mixture from step 2 above, paint the large surfaces of the roof.
9. Paint the edges of the roof in Light Chocolate.
10. Transfer checks onto the edges of the roof.
11. Mix 1 part Prairie Green and 1 part Soft Black and use mixture to paint squares on the roof edges. (Save this mixture to use later in the project.)
12. Transfer roof tiles onto the roof.
13. Paint roof tiles in Prairie Green, using Dry Brush Color technique and a light touch.
14. Transfer the windows, door, stoop, and sidewalk.
15. Using mixture from step 11 above, paint the windows.
16. Using mixture from step 2 above, paint the door.
17. Transfer remaining elements of pattern.
18. Paint house numbers and sidewalk in Burnt Umber.
19. Paint stoop and curtains in White Wash.
20. Add strokes of Ivory to each windowpane, using Dry Brush Color technique to produce a "glass" look.
21. Using mixture from step 2 above, paint the window trim.
22. Outline the door and paint the knob in Prairie Green.

Decorate the House
1. Apply floral design to each window in Prairie Green, using ¼″ stencil brush and Dry Brush Color technique.
2. Using wood end of brush, apply a random dot design to each floral in Light Seafoam Green.
3. Using wood end of brush, apply a random dot design to each floral with mixture from step 2 of "Paint the House."

WINDOW TRIM 6   FRONT

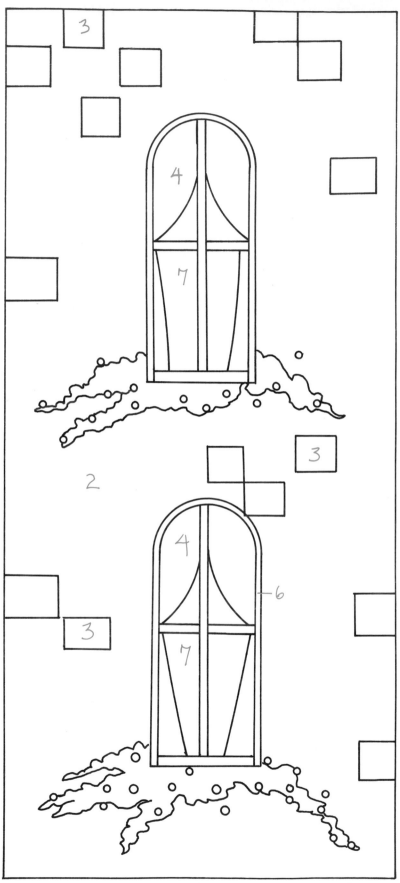

4. Using wood end of brush, apply a random dot design to each floral, first with Prairie Green, then Light Chocolate, and then White Wash.
5. Using Light Seafoam Green, add dots to the Prairie Green band around the house.
6. Apply wavy lines in Prairie Green and in Light Chocolate to the red band on the sidewalk.

Complete the Finishing Touches
1. Glue chimney to roof.
2. Apply antiquing mud. Allow to dry completely, at least 24 hours.
3. Sand to give an aged look (optional).
4. Using Outline-and-Paint technique, highlight curtains in White Wash.
5. Using Outline-and-Paint technique, highlight the greenery in Prairie Green.
6. Using Outline-and-Paint technique, highlight the door, with mixture from step 2 of "Paint the House."
7. Finish with 2 or 3 thin coats of varnish.

TALL VICTORIAN HOUSE BOX
1 PRAIRIE GREEN
2 LIGHT CHOCOLATE
3 BURNT UMBER
4 WHITE WASH
5 LIGHT SEAFOAM GREEN

Mixtures
6 JO SONJA RED + PRAIRIE GREEN
7 PRAIRIE GREEN + SOFT BLACK

SIDE

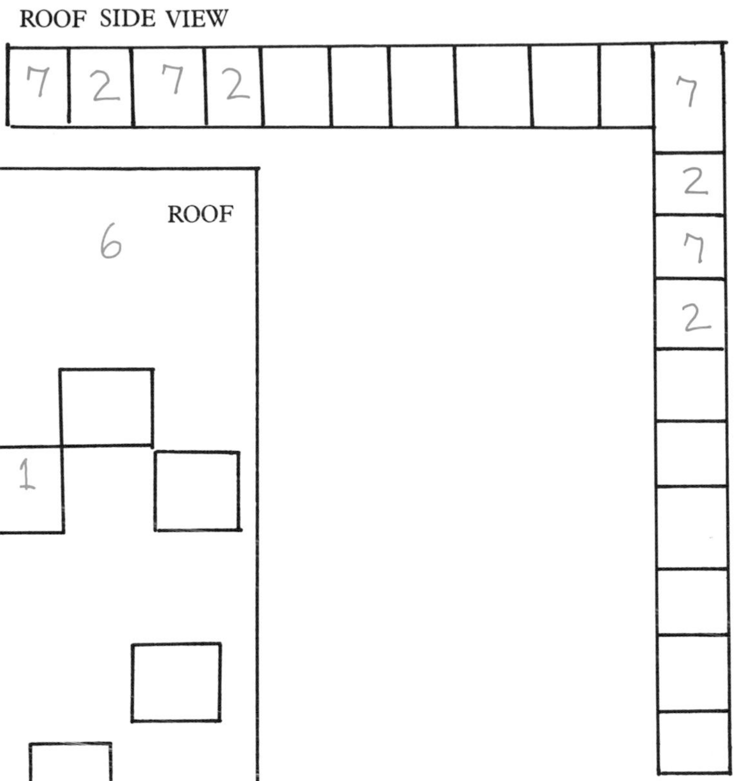
ROOF SIDE VIEW
7 2 7 2
7
2
7
2

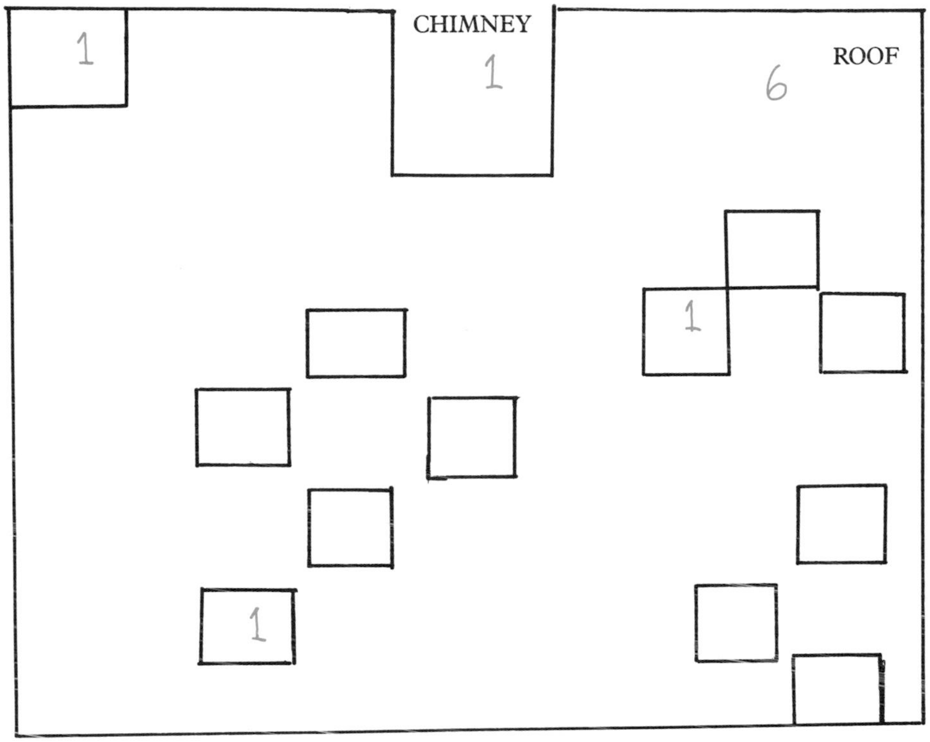
CHIMNEY
ROOF
1
1
6
1
1

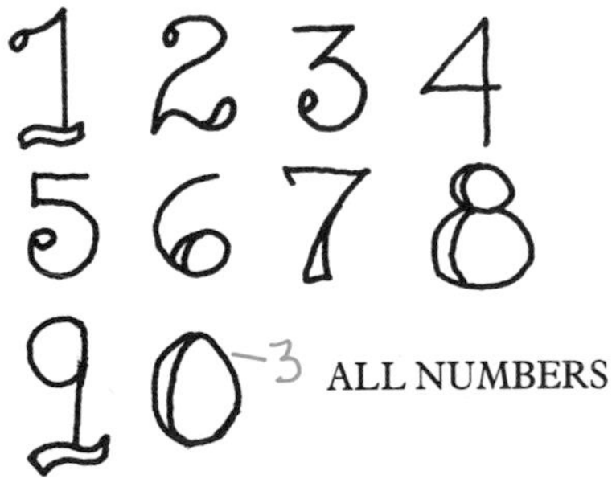
1 2 3 4
5 6 7 8
9 0
3
ALL NUMBERS

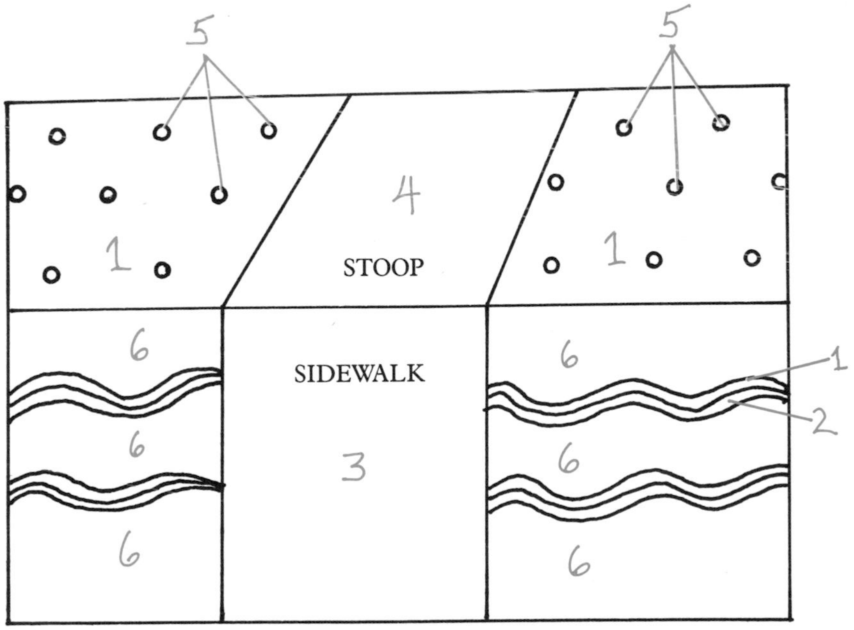
5
5
4
STOOP
1
1
6
SIDEWALK
6
1
2
6
3
6
6
6

Victorian House Recipe Box

This is a companion to the Tall Victorian House Box.
If you like to eat as much as we do, you probably
collect recipes. Our recipe box is a little gold mine of
special recipes printed on 3" × 5" cards by special friends.
Shown, page 100.

MATERIALS

Wooden recipe box
Sandpaper
Tack cloth
Sealer
Paper towels
Acrylic palette pad
Palette knife
Water containers
Antiquing mud (4-oz. jar) *or* Burnt Umber oil paint
1" polyfoam sponge brush
Brushes: #1 round; #8 *or* #10 flat; ¼" *or* ½" stencil
 brush

Pencil *or* marking pen
Graphite paper
Tracing paper
Drafting tape
Stylus
Eraser
Ruler
Wood glue *or* glue gun
Steel wool
Varnish

PALETTE

Delta Ceramcoat	*Jo Sonja Chroma*	*Illinois Bronze*
★	★	Prairie Green
Light Chocolate	Provincial Beige	Wicker
Burnt Umber	Brown Earth	Burnt Umber
Bright Red	Napthol Red Light	Jo Sonja Red
Black	Carbon Black	Soft Black
★	★	Light Seafoam Green
Ivory	Warm White	White Wash

DIRECTIONS

To prepare for this project, please read and follow the General Instructions and Basic Procedures for all projects (beginning on page 200) and the instructions for those particular Special Techniques used in this project (beginning on page 206).

Paint the House

1. Draw a horizontal line ½″ up from the bottom all around the house.
2. Paint the bottom ½″ of the house and the chimney in Prairie Green.
3. Paint the rest of the house in Light Chocolate.
4. Transfer bricks onto the house.
5. Paint bricks on the house in Burnt Umber very faintly, using Dry Brush Color technique.
6. Mix 5 parts Jo Sonja Red and ¼ part Prairie Green and use the mixture to paint the large surfaces of the roof. (Save this mixture to use later in the project.)
7. Paint the edges of the roof in Light Chocolate.
8. Transfer checks onto the edges of the roof, using roof pattern from Large Victorian House Box on page 103.
9. Mix 1 part Prairie Green and 1 part Soft Black and use mixture to paint the squares on the roof edges. (Save this mixture to use later in the project.)
10. Transfer roof tiles onto the roof randomly.
11. Paint roof tiles in Prairie Green, using the Dry Brush Color technique and a light touch.
12. Transfer the windows, door, and stoop.
13. Using mixture from step 9 above, paint the windows.
14. Using mixture from step 6 above, paint the door.
15. Transfer remaining elements of pattern.
16. Paint the stoop and curtains in White Wash.
17. Add strokes of White Wash to each windowpane, using the Dry Brush Color technique to produce a "glass" look.
18. Using mixture from step 6 above, paint the window trim.
19. Outline the door and paint the knob in Prairie Green.

VICTORIAN HOUSE RECIPE BOX
1 PRAIRIE GREEN
2 LIGHT CHOCOLATE
3 BURNT UMBER
4 WHITE WASH
5 LIGHT SEAFOAM GREEN

Mixtures
6 JO SONJA RED + PRAIRIE GREEN
7 PRAIRIE GREEN + SOFT BLACK

SIDE

Decorate the House

1. Apply floral design to each window in Prairie Green, using a ¼″ or ½″ stencil brush and Dry Brush Color technique.
2. Using wood end of brush, apply a random dot design to each floral in Light Seafoam Green.
3. Using wood end of brush, apply a random dot design to each floral, first with mixture from step 6 of "Paint the House," then Light Chocolate, and then White Wash.
4. Using Light Seafoam Green, add dots to the Prairie Green band around the house.

Complete the Finishing Touches

1. Glue chimney to roof.
2. Apply antiquing mud. Allow to dry completely, at least 24 hours.
3. Sand to give an aged look (optional).
4. Using Outline-and-Paint technique, highlight the curtains in White Wash.
5. Using Outline-and-Paint technique, highlight the greenery in Prairie Green.
6. Using Outline-and-Paint technique, highlight the door, with mixture from step 6 of "Paint the House."
7. Finish with 2 or 3 thin coats of varnish.

FRONT

Little Victorian Cottage Box

*I'm a pushover for items that even suggest they'll help me
to get organized. This box will house
small objects—paper clips, twist ties, thumbtacks, or tea bags.
The tall Victorian box and the recipe box,
along with this little box, make a nice
kitchen group. Shown, page 100.*

MATERIALS

Wooden cottage kit
Sandpaper
Tack cloth
Sealer
Paper towels
Acrylic palette pad
Palette knife
Water containers
Antiquing mud (4-oz. jar) *or* Burnt Umber oil paint
Linseed oil/mineral spirits
1″ polyfoam sponge brush
Brushes: #8 flat; #1 round

Pencil *or* marking pen
White transfer paper
Tracing paper
Drafting tape
Ruler
Eraser
Wood glue *or* glue gun
Steel wool
Varnish

PALETTE

Delta Ceramcoat	*Jo Sonja Chroma*	*Illinois Bronze*
Light Chocolate	Provincial Beige	Wicker
Bright Red	Napthol Red Light	Jo Sonja Red
Black	Carbon Black	Soft Black
Woodland Night	★	Prairie Green
Light Ivory	Warm White	White Wash

DIRECTIONS

To prepare for this project, please read and follow the General Instructions and Basic Procedures for all projects (beginning on page 200) and the instructions for those particular Special Techniques used in this project (beginning on page 206).

Paint and Decorate the Cottage

1. Draw a horizontal line ⁵⁄₁₆″ up from the bottom all around the cottage.
2. Paint the bottom ⁵⁄₁₆″ in Prairie Green.
3. Paint the rest of the cottage in Light Chocolate.
4. Paint the large surfaces of the roof in Prairie Green.
5. Paint the edges of the roof in Light Chocolate.
6. Pencil checks on the edges at ³⁄₈″ intervals.
7. Mix 1 part Soft Black and 1 part Prairie Green and use mixture to paint alternate squares on roof edges.
8. Transfer the details of the cottage.
9. Mix 2 parts Jo Sonja Red and ⅛ part Prairie Green and use mixture to paint chimneys and door.
10. Paint windows using mixture from step 7, above.
11. Paint the trim around the door using mixture from step 7, above.
12. Paint the trim around the windows using mixture from step 9, above.
13. Paint the front stoop in White Wash.

Complete the Finishing Touches

1. Glue on chimneys.
2. Apply antiquing mud. Allow to dry completely, at least 24 hours.
3. Finish with 2 thin coats of varnish.

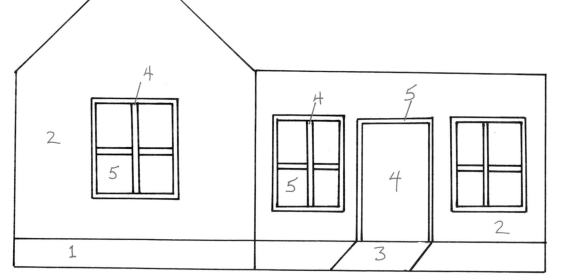

LITTLE VICTORIAN COTTAGE BOX
1 PRAIRIE GREEN
2 LIGHT CHOCOLATE
3 WHITE WASH

Mixtures
4 JO SONJA RED + PRAIRIE GREEN
5 PRAIRIE GREEN + SOFT BLACK

Rowhouse Bed-and-Breakfast Tray

When I saw this tray, it evoked memories of a trip to England.
The English rowhouse doors are painted the richest colors
I have ever seen on homes. Use this tray for breakfast in bed
or to serve afternoon tea to a friend…
Don't forget the tea cakes, brown sugar, fresh clotted cream,
and strawberry jam. Place a lovely heirloom napkin
across your lap and enjoy the moment.

MATERIALS

Wooden tray
Sandpaper
Tack cloth
Sealer
Paper towels
Acrylic palette pad
Palette knife
Water containers
Linseed oil/mineral spirits
1″ polyfoam sponge brush
Antiquing mud (4-oz. jar) *or* Burnt Umber oil paint
Brushes: #8 *or* #10 flat; #1 round

Pencil *or* marking pen
Graphite paper
Tracing paper
Drafting tape
Stylus
Eraser
Steel wool
Varnish

PALETTE

Delta Ceramcoat	*Jo Sonja Chroma*	*Illinois Bronze*
Tomato Spice	Red Earth	Jo Sonja Red
Straw	Yellow Oxide	Golden Harvest
Woodland Night	★	Prairie Green
Liberty Blue	★	★
Pumpkin	★	True Orange
Colonial Blue	Aqua	Marina Blue
Dresden Flesh	★	★
Black	Carbon Black	Soft Black
White	Titanium White	White Wash

DIRECTIONS

To prepare for this project, please read and follow the General Instructions and Basic Procedures for all projects (beginning on page 200) and the instructions for those particular Special Techniques used in this project (beginning on page 206).

Paint the Tray and the Houses

1. Paint the underside and the inside of the tray and the handle in Dresden Flesh.
2. Transfer the general outline of each house. Move pattern as needed to complete all the houses. (Details will be transferred later.)
3. Paint the chimneys in Soft Black.
4. Mix 5 parts Prairie Green and ½ part Dresden Flesh and use the mixture to paint the roofs on all #1 houses and #5 houses. (Save this mixture to use later in the project.)
5. Paint all #1 houses and #5 houses in True Orange.
6. Paint the roofs on all #2 houses and #4 houses in Jo Sonja Red.
7. Paint all #2 houses and #4 houses in Golden Harvest.
8. Paint the roofs of all #3 houses in Marina Blue.
9. Paint all #3 houses in Liberty Blue.

Transfer and Paint House Details

1. Transfer the details of the houses.
2. Paint all the windows in White Wash.
3. Outline the windows in Soft Black.
4. Paint the doors on all #1 houses and #5 houses in Marina Blue.
5. Paint the doorknobs on all #1 houses and #5 houses in True Orange.
6. Paint the doors on all #2 houses and #4 houses in Jo Sonja Red.
7. Paint the doorknobs on all #2 houses and #4 houses in Golden Harvest.
8. Paint the doors on all #3 houses in True Orange.
9. Using mixture from step 4 of "Paint the Tray and Houses," paint the doorknobs on all #3 houses.
10. Outline all the doors in Soft Black.

Complete the Finishing Touches

1. Apply antiquing mud. Allow to dry completely, at least 24 hours.
2. Finish with 2 thin coats of varnish.

DIAGRAM FOR A/C SIDES

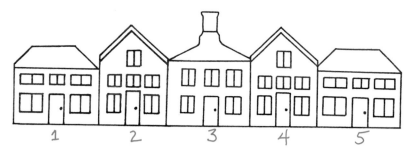

DIAGRAM FOR B/D SIDES

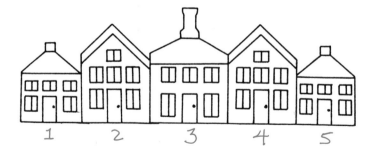

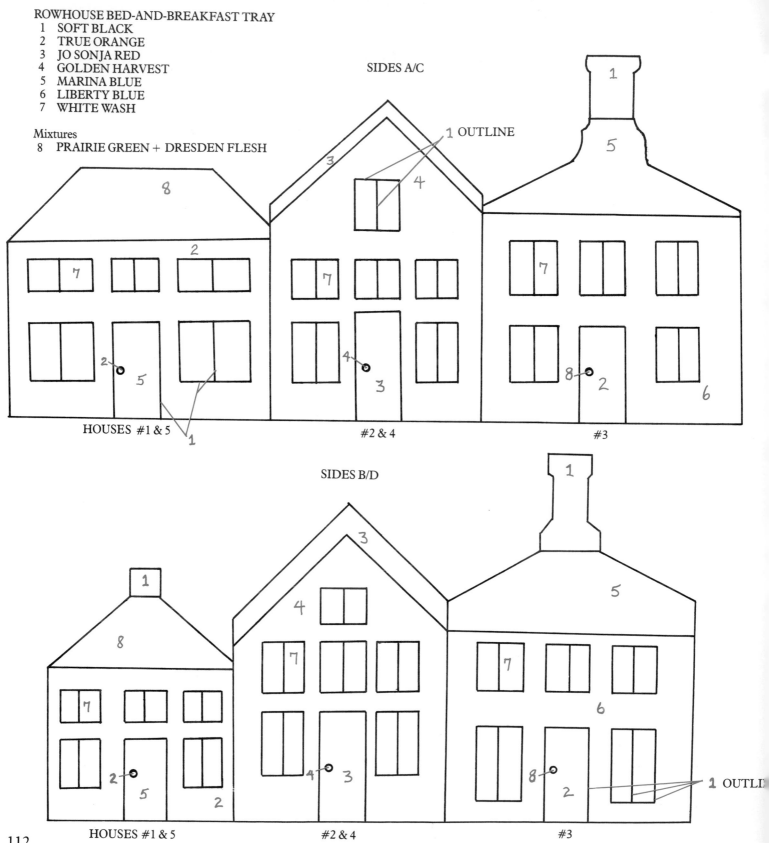

ROWHOUSE BED-AND-BREAKFAST TRAY
1 SOFT BLACK
2 TRUE ORANGE
3 JO SONJA RED
4 GOLDEN HARVEST
5 MARINA BLUE
6 LIBERTY BLUE
7 WHITE WASH

Mixtures
8 PRAIRIE GREEN + DRESDEN FLESH

SIDES A/C

1 OUTLINE

HOUSES #1 & 5   #2 & 4   #3

SIDES B/D

1 OUTLI

HOUSES #1 & 5   #2 & 4   #3

112

Fresh Fruit Refrigerator Magnets

*If your house is like ours, there's always plenty of material
to hang on the refrigerator. Use this magnet collection
on the fridge, or if you prefer, attach hangers to the backs
and display in a grouping someplace that needs brightening.*

MATERIALS

Wooden *refrigerator* magnets (fruit shapes)
Sandpaper
Tack cloth
Sealer
Paper towels
Acrylic palette pad
Palette knife
Water containers
Brushes: #1 round; #8 *or* #10 flat; ¼″ *or* ½″ stencil
  brush
Small piece of natural sponge

Pencil *or* marking pen
Graphite paper
Tracing paper
Drafting tape
Stylus
Eraser
Steel wool
Varnish

PALETTE

Delta Ceramcoat	*Jo Sonja Chroma*	*Illinois Bronze*
Bright Red	Napthol Red Light	Jo Sonja Red
Mendocino	Burgundy	Bordeaux
White	Titanium White	Soft White
Burnt Umber	Brown Earth	Burnt Umber
Salem Green	Teal Green + Warm White	Telemark Green
Colonial Blue	Aqua	Marina Blue
Black	Carbon Black	Soft Black
Straw	★	Golden Harvest
Georgia Clay	Norwegian Orange	Pennsylvania Clay

DIRECTIONS

To prepare for this project, please read and follow the General Instructions and Basic Procedures for all projects (beginning on page 200) and the instructions for those particular Special Techniques used in this project (beginning on page 206).

Paint the Apple

1. Paint apple in Jo Sonja Red.
2. Shade one side of apple in Bordeaux, using stencil brush and Dry Brush Color technique.
3. Highlight opposite side of apple in Soft White, using stencil brush and Dry Brush Color technique.
4. Paint stem in Burnt Umber.

Transfer and Paint the Melon

1. Transfer general outline to melon.
2. Mix 2 parts Jo Sonja Red and 1 part Soft White and use mixture to paint meat of the melon.
3. Paint rind in Soft White.
4. Paint skin in Telemark Green. Then, while Telemark Green is damp, paint diagonal markings on outside rind in Soft White.
5. Transfer seeds.
6. Paint seeds in Soft Black.
7. Using natural sponge and Sponge Painting technique, lightly apply Bordeaux on top of melon.

Paint the Plum

1. Mix 2 parts Marina Blue and 2 parts Bordeaux and use mixture to paint plum.
2. Add ⅛ part Soft Black to the mixture in step 1 and use it to shade plum.
3. Paint stem in Soft Black.
4. Paint tip of stem in Telemark Green.
5. Mix 1 part Soft White and 1 part Marina Blue and use mixture to highlight one side of the plum close to the cleavage line. (Refer to photo.)

Transfer and Paint the Grapes

1. Transfer details to grapes.
2. Paint leaves in Telemark Green.
3. Transfer veins onto leaves.
4. Paint veins and stem in Soft Black.
5. Paint tip of stem in Burnt Umber.
6. Mix ¼ part Telemark Green and ¼ part Soft Black and use mixture to shade leaves.
7. Paint entire grape area in Bordeaux.
8. Mix 1 part Soft White and 1 part Bordeaux. Dip your little or index finger in the mixture, blot lightly on paper towel, and apply paint to wood piece. Practice on paper a few times until you regularly get a nice, full, round grape shape. Repeat for each grape. Highlight grapes randomly in soft white.

Paint the Pear

1. Paint pear in Golden Harvest.
2. Using Dry Brush Color technique, highlight both sides of pear in Pennsylvania Clay.
3. Shade one side of pear (over Pennsylvania Clay) in Bordeaux.
4. Highlight other side of pear using Soft White. (Refer to photo.)
5. Paint stem of pear in Burnt Umber.
6. Add a few strokes to blossom end of pear in Burnt Umber.
7. Add 3 or 5 tiny dots to blossom end of pear in Soft White.

Complete the Finishing Touches

1. Finish all five pieces with 2 thin coats of varnish.

Pick up
Elisabeth
at Ballet
2:00

Buy more
Paint !

MILK
EGGS
BREAD
CHEESE
PASTA

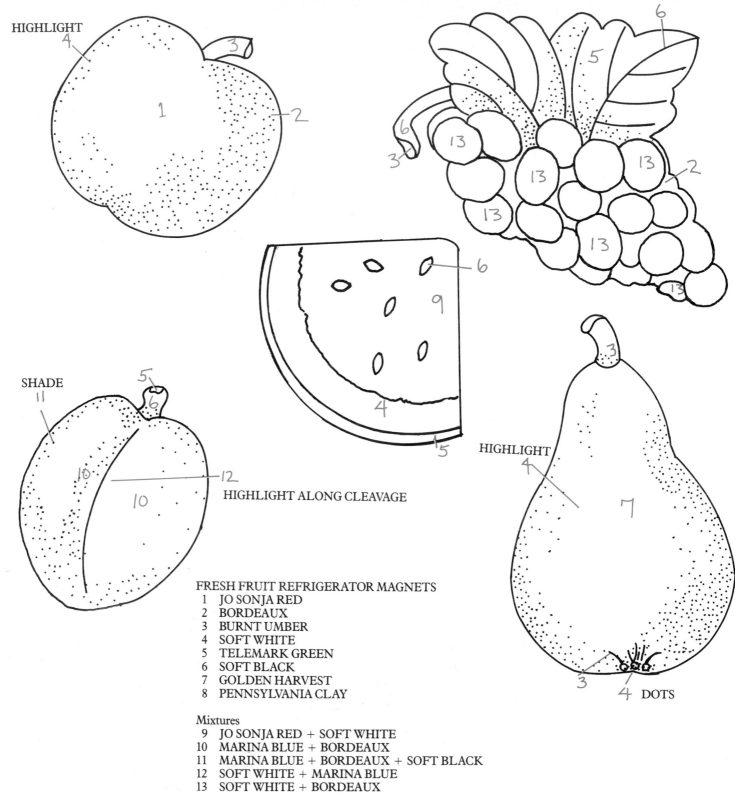

HIGHLIGHT

SHADE

HIGHLIGHT ALONG CLEAVAGE

HIGHLIGHT

DOTS

FRESH FRUIT REFRIGERATOR MAGNETS
1   JO SONJA RED
2   BORDEAUX
3   BURNT UMBER
4   SOFT WHITE
5   TELEMARK GREEN
6   SOFT BLACK
7   GOLDEN HARVEST
8   PENNSYLVANIA CLAY

Mixtures
9   JO SONJA RED + SOFT WHITE
10 MARINA BLUE + BORDEAUX
11 MARINA BLUE + BORDEAUX + SOFT BLACK
12 SOFT WHITE + MARINA BLUE
13 SOFT WHITE + BORDEAUX
14 TELEMARK GREEN + SOFT BLACK

Country Vanity

Victorian Pegboard Shelf

When I was young I was taught, "A place for everything and everything in its place," and I'm still incorporating the concept into my life. With this perennially useful adage in mind, attach this shelf under a medicine cabinet, over a towel bar, next to a mirror, or wherever you need a "place for something."

MATERIALS

Wooden shelf and heart embellishments
Sandpaper
Tack cloth
Sealer
Paper towels
Acrylic palette pad
Palette knife
Water containers
1″ polyfoam sponge brush
Antiquing mud (4-oz. jar) *or* Burnt Umber oil paint
Linseed oil/mineral spirits
Small piece of natural sponge
Brushes: #1 round; #8 flat

Wood glue *or* glue gun
Steel wool
Varnish

PALETTE

Delta Ceramcoat	*Jo Sonja Chroma*	*Illinois Bronze*
Dark Night	Storm Blue	Liberty Blue
Kim Gold	Rich Gold	★
Wedgewood Blue	★	★
★	★	Light Seafoam Green
Empire Gold	Turner's Yellow	Dijon Gold
Mendocino	Burgundy	Bordeaux
★	★	Apache Red

DIRECTIONS

To prepare for this project, please read and follow the General Instructions and Basic Procedures for all projects (beginning on page 200) and the instructions for those particular Special Techniques used in this project (beginning on page 206).

Paint the Shelf and Hearts

1. Paint entire shelf and pegs in Liberty Blue.
2. Using natural sponge and Sponge Painting technique, apply Rich Gold to all visible surfaces of shelf and ends of pegs.
3. Apply freehand striping to shelf and brackets in Wedgewood Blue. (Refer to pattern.)
4. Add narrow linework next to both sides of Wedgewood Blue striping in Light Seafoam Green.
5. Paint one heart in Bordeaux.
6. Paint the same heart in Apache Red.
7. Paint second heart in Dijon Gold.

Complete the Finishing Touches

1. Glue in pegs.
2. Apply antiquing mud to shelf and hearts. Allow to dry completely, at least 24 hours.
3. Use Sanding to Age technique to randomly and lightly highlight shelf.
4. Use Outline-and-Paint technique to highlight linework, if needed.
5. Finish with 2 thin coats of varnish.

½ PATTERN   CENTER

HEART A: 5, 6
HEART B: 7

VICTORIAN PEGBOARD SHELF
1 LIBERTY BLUE
2 RICH GOLD
3 WEDGEWOOD BLUE
4 LIGHT SEAFOAM GREEN
5 BORDEAUX
6 APACHE RED
7 DIJON GOLD

CENTER

Victorian Heart Jewelry Box

*I painted this box for my mother, whose favorite color is blue
and who likes all things Victorian. In fact,
this entire collection was designed with her in mind.
It makes a delightful gift for a special Mothers' Day.
Shown, page 117.*

MATERIALS

Wooden heart box
Sandpaper
Tack cloth
Sealer
Paper towels
Acrylic palette pad
Palette knife
Water containers
1″ polyfoam sponge brush
Antiquing mud (4-oz. jar) *or* Burnt Umber oil paint
Linseed oil/mineral spirits
Brushes: #3 round; #5 round; #8 *or* #10 flat

Pencil *or* marking pen
White transfer paper
Tracing paper
Drafting tape
Stylus
Eraser
Steel wool
Varnish

PALETTE

Delta Ceramcoat	*Jo Sonja Chroma*	*Illinois Bronze*
Kim Gold	Rich Gold	★
Liberty Blue	★	★
Wedgewood Blue	★	★
Empire Gold	Turner's Yellow	Dijon Gold
Black	Carbon Black	Soft Black
★	★	Apache Red
★	★	Light Seafoam Green
Mendocino	Burgundy	Bordeaux

DIRECTIONS

To prepare for this project, please read and follow the General Instructions and Basic Procedures for all projects (beginning on page 200) and the instructions for those particular Special Techniques used in this project (beginning on page 206).

Paint the Box

1. Paint entire box in Liberty Blue.
2. Transfer outline of inner heart, linework on edge of lid, and alternating stripes on the sides of the box.
3. Paint inner heart and stripes on the sides of box in one coat of Wedgewood Blue.
4. Paint narrow, vertical lines in Light Seafoam Green to outline each stripe. (Refer to photo.)
5. Add 3 dots in Light Seafoam Green to each blue stripe that does not have a leaf design.
6. Paint narrow band in Light Seafoam Green onto bottom edge of each stripe with leaf design. (Refer to photo.)

Transfer and Paint the Decorative Details

1. Transfer the linework and details.
2. Paint the linework on the lid in Rich Gold.
3. Paint the leaf design on alternate stripes of the box sides in Rich Gold.
4. Outline the outer heart in Wedgewood Blue.
5. Paint the lined leaves on the lid in Soft Black.
6. Paint all the other leaves in Light Seafoam Green.
7. Paint red roses in Bordeaux.
8. Paint red roses in Apache Red.
9. Mix 1 part Bordeaux and 1/10 part Soft Black and use mixture to shade red roses.
10. Add a dot to the center of each red rose in Dijon Gold.
11. Paint yellow roses in Dijon Gold.
12. Shade yellow roses in Bordeaux.
13. Add a dot to center of each yellow rose in Apache Red.
14. Outline the inner heart in Rich Gold.
15. Add linework to heart in Rich Gold.
16. Add Light Seafoam Green linework to heart.
17. Add dot design to heart, first in Light Seafoam Green, then in Rich Gold, and finally, in Apache Red.
18. Paint 2 tiny hearts on floral design in Dijon Gold.
19. Paint 1 tiny heart on floral design in Apache Red.

Complete the Finishing Touches

1. Sand the box gently to age it.
2. Apply antiquing mud. Allow to dry completely, at least 24 hours.
3. Using Sanding to Highlight technique, lightly highlight box.
4. Using Outline-and-Paint technique, highlight red roses in Apache red.
5. Using Outline-and-Paint technique, highlight yellow roses in Dijon Gold.
6. Using Outline-and-Paint technique, highlight randomly selected green leaves in Light Seafoam Green.
7. Using Outline-and-Paint technique, highlight randomly selected gold linework in Rich Gold.
8. Using Outline-and-Paint technique, highlight randomly selected green linework in Light Seafoam Green.
9. Finish with 2 thin coats of varnish.

LID

VICTORIAN HEART JEWELRY BOX
1 LIBERTY BLUE
2 RICH GOLD
3 WEDGEWOOD BLUE
4 LIGHT SEAFOAM GREEN
5 DIJON GOLD
6 SOFT BLACK
7 BORDEAUX
8 APACHE RED

Mixtures
9 BORDEAUX + SOFT BLACK

BOX SIDE STRIPES

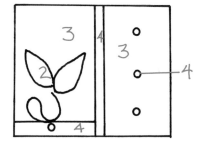

LID EDGE

122

Victorian Dispenser Cover

A hand-painted container to hide a commercial plastic soap or lotion dispenser is an added touch of coordinated country decor to this ensemble. A handy tip from my husband's side of the family: Save those tiny chips from bar soaps, add water, and make your own liquid soap.
Shown, page 117.

MATERIALS

Wooden dispenser cover
Sandpaper
Tack cloth
Sealer
Paper towels
Acrylic palette pad
Palette knife
Water containers
1" polyfoam sponge brush
Antiquing mud (4-oz. jar) *or* Burnt Umber oil paint
Linseed oil/mineral spirits
Small piece of natural sponge
Brushes: #1 and #3 round; #8 *or* #10 flat

Pencil *or* marking pen
White transfer paper
Tracing paper
Drafting tape
Stylus
Eraser
Ruler
Steel wool
Varnish

PALETTE

Delta Ceramcoat	*Jo Sonja Chroma*	*Illinois Bronze*
Kim Gold	Rich Gold	★
Liberty Blue	★	★
Wedgewood Blue	★	★
Empire Gold	Turner's Yellow	Dijon Gold
Black	Carbon Black	Soft Black
★	★	Apache Red
★	★	Light Seafoam Green
Mendocino	Burgundy	Bordeaux

DIRECTIONS

To prepare for this project, please read and follow the General Instructions and Basic Procedures for all projects (beginning on page 200) and the instructions for those particular Special Techniques used in this project (beginning on page 206).

Paint the Dispenser Cover and Heart

1. Paint dispenser cover in Liberty Blue.
2. Using natural sponge and Sponge Painting technique, apply Rich Gold over blue basecoat. (Refer to pattern and avoid areas reserved for heart and stripes.)
3. Transfer outline of heart and stripes onto the front, sides, and top of dispenser.
4. Paint stripes on side, top, and bottom edges of dispenser in one coat of Wedgewood Blue.
5. Paint heart in one coat of Wedgewood Blue.
6. Outline each stripe in a narrow line of Light Seafoam Green.
7. Outline heart in Rich Gold.
8. Add Rich Gold linework to heart.
9. Add Light Seafoam Green linework to heart. (Refer to photo.)

Transfer and Paint the Floral Design

1. Transfer remaining elements of pattern to dispenser cover.
2. Paint lined leaves in Black.
3. Paint remaining leaves in Light Seafoam Green.
4. Paint red roses in Bordeaux.
5. Paint Bordeaux roses in Apache Red.
6. Mix 3 parts Bordeaux and ½ part Soft Black and use mixture to shade red roses.
7. Add a dot to the center of each red rose in Dijon Gold.
8. Paint yellow roses in Dijon Gold.
9. Shade yellow roses in Apache Red.

Complete the Finishing Touches

1. Gently sand dispenser cover to age it.
2. Apply antiquing mud. Allow to dry completely, at least 24 hours.
3. Use Sanding to Highlight technique, highlight the dispenser.

4. Using Outline-and-Paint technique, highlight red roses in Apache Red. (Refer to photo.)
5. Using Outline-and-Paint technique, highlight yellow roses in Dijon Gold. (Refer to photo.)
6. Using Outline-and-Paint technique, highlight randomly selected green leaves in Light Seafoam Green. (Refer to photo.)
7. Using Outline-and-Paint technique, highlight randomly selected gold linework in Rich Gold. (Refer to photo.)
8. Using Outline-and-Paint technique, highlight randomly selected green linework in Light Seafoam Green. (Refer to photo.)
9. Finish with 2 thin coats of varnish.

SIDE

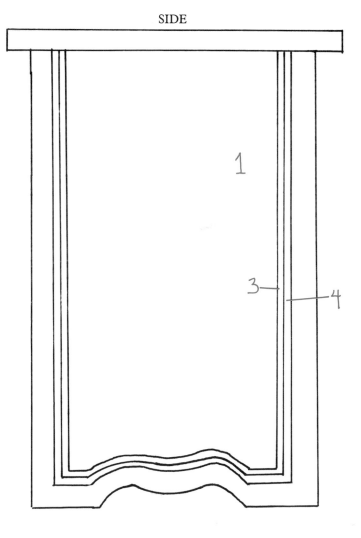

VICTORIAN DISPENSER COVER
1 LIBERTY BLUE
2 RICH GOLD
3 WEDGEWOOD BLUE
4 LIGHT SEAFOAM GREEN
5 SOFT BLACK
6 BORDEAUX
7 APACHE RED
8 DIJON GOLD

Mixtures
9 BORDEAUX + SOFT BLACK

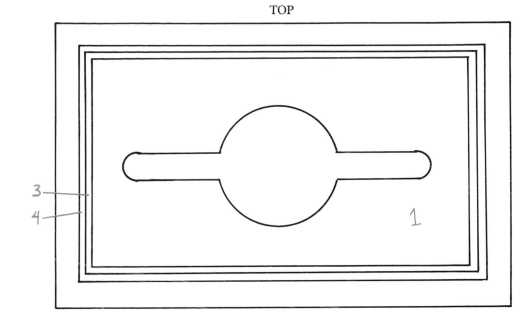

TOP

FRONT

Victorian Tissue Box Cover

Adding further interest to this pretty ensemble, this tissue box cover turns a functional but mundane object into a lovely accessory. The color scheme offers a range of hues on which to base the decor of the whole room, if you like.

MATERIALS

Wooden tissue box cover
Sandpaper
Tack cloth
Sealer
Paper towels
Acrylic palette pad
Water containers
1″ polyfoam sponge brush
Antiquing mud (4-oz. jar) *or* Burnt Umber oil paint
Linseed oil/mineral spirits
Wood stain (optional, or make your own)
Scruffy old toothbrush *or* stencil brush
Brushes: #1 round; #3 round; #8 flat

Pencil *or* marking pen
White transfer paper
Tracing paper
Drafting tape
Stylus
Eraser
Steel wool
Varnish

PALETTE

Delta Ceramcoat	*Jo Sonja Chroma*	*Illinois Bronze*
White	Titanium White	Soft White
Kim Gold	Rich Gold	★
Liberty Blue	★	★
Wedgewood Blue	★	★
Empire Gold	Turner's Yellow	Dijon Gold
Black	Carbon Black	Soft Black
★	★	Apache Red
Mendocino	Burgundy	Bordeaux
★	★	Light Seafoam Green

DIRECTIONS

To prepare for this project, please read and follow the General Instructions and Basic Procedures for all projects (beginning on page 200) and the instructions for those particular Special Techniques used in this project (beginning on page 206).

Paint the Box and Floral Design

1. Paint entire box in Liberty Blue.
2. Transfer floral and bottom border patterns to box. (Veins in leaves will be transferred later.)
3. Paint bottom border in Wedgewood Blue.
4. Outline border in Light Seafoam Green.
5. Outline green outline in Rich Gold.
6. Add dot design to blue border in Rich Gold.
7. Outline opening of box in Rich Gold.
8. Paint leaves marked on pattern with lines in Soft Black.
9. Paint remaining leaves in Light Seafoam Green.
10. Paint red roses in Apache Red.
11. Shade red roses in Bordeaux.
12. Add a dot to center of each red rose in Dijon Gold.
13. Paint yellow roses in Dijon Gold.
14. Shade yellow roses in Apache Red.
15. Add a dot to the center of each yellow rose in Soft White.
16. Add linework in Rich Gold.
17. Add dot design to center of yellow flowers in Soft White. (Refer to pattern.)
18. Add dot design randomly among leaves in Light Seafoam Green.
19. Add Rich Gold dots among Rich Gold linework.

Complete the Finishing Touches

1. Sand the box gently to age it.
2. Apply antiquing mud. Allow to dry completely, at least 24 hours.
3. Using Sanding to Highlight technique, highlight box randomly.
4. Spatter entire box first in Light Seafoam Green and then in Rich Gold.
5. Mix 2 tablespoons mineral spirits and 1 tablespoon antiquing mud and use mixture to stain the inside of the box (optional).
6. Finish with 2 thin coats of varnish.

127

LEFT SIDE

RIGHT SIDE

BOX FRONT

BOTTOM BORDER

REFER TO PHOTO FOR PLACEMENT

VICTORIAN TISSUE BOX COVER
1 LIBERTY BLUE
2 WEDGEWOOD BLUE
3 LIGHT SEAFOAM GREEN
4 RICH GOLD
5 SOFT BLACK
6 APACHE RED
7 BORDEAUX
8 DIJON GOLD
9 SOFT WHITE

128

Victorian Wastebasket

*Of all the functional accessories, this wastebasket is especially
gratifying to embellish. Your efforts will transform
an object which doesn't usually get much attention
into a truly beautiful hand-painted treasure.*

MATERIALS

Wooden wastebasket
Sandpaper
Tack cloth
Sealer
Paper towels
Acrylic palette pad
Palette knife
Water containers
1″ polyfoam sponge brush
Antiquing mud (4-oz. jar) *or* Burnt Umber oil paint
Linseed oil/mineral spirits
Small piece of natural sponge
Brushes: #3 round; #5 round; #8 *or* #10 flat

Pencil *or* marking pen
White transfer paper
Tracing paper
Drafting tape
Stylus
Eraser
Ruler
Steel wool
Varnish

PALETTE

Delta Ceramcoat	*Jo Sonja Chroma*	*Illinois Bronze*
Kim Gold	Rich Gold	★
Liberty Blue	★	★
Wedgewood Blue	★	★
Black	Carbon Black	Soft Black
★	★	Apache Red
★	★	Light Seafoam Green
Mendocino	Burgundy	Bordeaux
Empire Gold	Turner's Yellow	Dijon Gold

DIRECTIONS

To prepare for this project, please read and follow the General Instructions and Basic Procedures for all projects (beginning on page 200) and the instructions for those particular Special Techniques used in this project (beginning on page 206).

Paint the Wastebasket and Heart Pattern

1. Paint entire wastebasket in Liberty Blue.
2. Using natural sponge and Sponge Painting technique, apply Rich Gold to Liberty Blue areas. (Refer to pattern and avoid areas where the heart and the borders will be.)
3. Transfer outline of heart to front of wastebasket.
4. Paint heart in Wedgewood Blue.
5. Paint ½" striping following the contours of all edges of wastebasket in Wedgewood Blue.
6. Outline Wedgewood Blue border in Light Seafoam Green.
7. Add petal strokes to each corner in Light Seafoam Green.

Transfer and Paint the Floral Details

1. Transfer leaf and floral design to heart.
2. Paint lined leaves in Soft Black.
3. Paint all other leaves in Light Seafoam Green.
4. Using Floated Color technique, paint red roses in Bordeaux.
5. Paint Bordeaux roses in Apache Red.
6. Mix 3 parts Bordeaux and ½ part Soft Black and use mixture to shade red roses.
7. Add a dot to center of each red rose in Dijon Gold.
8. Paint yellow roses in Dijon Gold.
9. Using Floated Color technique, shade yellow roses in Apache Red.
10. Add a dot to the center of each yellow rose in Apache Red.

Paint the Heart Details

1. Outline heart in Rich Gold.
2. Add Rich Gold linework to heart.
3. Add Light Seafoam Green linework to heart. (Refer to photo.)
4. Add dot design to heart—first in Light Seafoam Green, then in Rich Gold, and finally, in Apache Red.
5. Paint 2 tiny hearts on floral design in Dijon Gold.
6. Paint 1 tiny heart on floral design in Apache Red.

Complete the Finishing Touches

1. Sand the wastebasket gently to age it.
2. Apply antiquing mud. Allow to dry completely, at least 24 hours.
3. Using Sanding to Highlight technique to sand the basket very lightly and randomly.
4. Using Outline-and-Paint technique, highlight red roses randomly in Apache Red.
5. Using Outline-and-Paint technique, highlight yellow roses randomly in Dijon Gold.
6. Using Outline-and-Paint technique, highlight randomly selected green leaves and green linework in Light Seafoam Green.
7. Using Outline-and-Paint technique, highlight randomly selected gold linework in Rich Gold.
8. Finish with 2 thin coats of varnish.

CENTER

CENTER

TER

CENTER

VICTORIAN WASTEBASKET
1 LIBERTY BLUE
2 RICH GOLD
3 WEDGEWOOD BLUE
4 LIGHT SEAFOAM GREEN
5 SOFT BLACK
6 BORDEAUX
7 APACHE RED
8 DIJON GOLD

PETAL STROKES
ADD TO EACH CORNER OF BASKET

131

Petit Fleur Grandfather Clock

*The lines of this clock—very feminine and appealing—help
make it my favorite piece. It evokes memories of reading
a book of Emily Dickinson's poems for the first time,
a pretty volume illustrated with billowing satin gowns and
lace gloves and curtains, and afternoon teas.*

MATERIALS

Wooden clock kit with mechanism and dial face
Sandpaper
Tack cloth
Sealer
Paper towels
Acrylic palette pad
Palette knife
Water containers
1″ polyfoam sponge brush
Antiquing mud (4-oz. jar) *or* Burnt Umber oil paint
Small piece of natural sponge
Brushes: #1 round; #3 round; #6 flat

Pencil *or* marking pen
Graphite paper
Tracing paper
Drafting tape
Stylus
Eraser
Spray adhesive
Steel wool
Varnish

PALETTE

Delta Ceramcoat	*Jo Sonja Chroma*	*Illinois Bronze*
Kim Gold	Rich Gold	★
White	Titanium White	Soft White
Bright Red	Napthol Red Light	Jo Sonja Red
Bright Yellow	Cadmium Yellow Mid "C"	Sunkiss Yellow
Black	Carbon Black	Soft Black
Green Isle	Brilliant Green	Holiday Green
Terra Cotta + White	★	L'Orangerie

DIRECTIONS

To prepare for this project, please read and follow the General Instructions and Basic Procedures for all projects (beginning on page 200) and the instructions for those particular Special Techniques used in this project (beginning on page 206).

Paint the Clock

1. Paint entire clock in Soft White, except dial face area, which will not be painted at all.
2. Paint hinges in Rich Gold.
3. Using a natural sponge and Sponge Painting technique apply Rich Gold to entire clock with a light touch.
4. Paint more Rich Gold on selected areas: knob, top molding, bottom molding, frame of dial face, and shelf facings. (Refer to photo.)

Transfer and Paint the Floral Design

1. Transfer floral design to clock body and 3-petal design to four corners of dial face.
2. Mix 2 parts Soft White, 2 parts Jo Sonja Red, and 1/10 part Sunkiss Yellow and use mixture to paint roses.
3. Shade roses in Jo Sonja Red.
4. Paint dotted leaves on pattern in Soft Black.
5. Mix 4 parts Holiday Green, 2 parts Sunkiss Yellow, 1/10 part Jo Sonja Red, and 1/8 part L'Orangerie and use mixture to paint remaining leaves.
6. Using mixture from step 5 above, paint tendrils.
7. Paint dots in center of roses in Soft White.
8. Using mixtures from steps 2 and 5 above, alternately apply random dots among floral designs.
9. Paint 3-petal designs in corners in Rich Gold.

Complete the Finishing Touches

1. Apply antiquing mud. Allow to dry completely, at least 24 hours. Remember to antique inside of door and shelving.
2. Install dial face following kit instructions.
3. Finish with 2 or 3 thin coats of varnish.
4. Install clock mechanism following kit instructions.

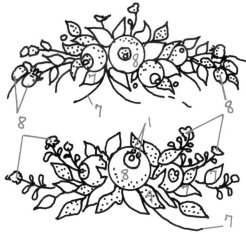

CORNERS OF DIAL FACE

PETIT FLEUR GRANDFATHER CLOCK
1 SOFT WHITE
2 JO SONJA RED
3 SUNKISS YELLOW
4 SOFT BLACK
5 HOLIDAY GREEN
6 RICH GOLD

Mixtures
7 HOLIDAY GREEN + SUNKISS YELLOW
   + JO SONJA RED + L'ORANGERIE
8 SOFT WHITE + JO SONJA RED
   + SUNKISS YELLOW

Country Manor Bookends

*This fun and easy-to-paint set is practical too.
That increases its appeal for me
since I like anything that promises to help me
get organized—and adds a touch of country warmth
to my home at the same time.*

MATERIALS
Wooden bookends kit
Sandpaper
Tack cloth
Sealer
Paper towels
Acrylic palette pad
Palette knife
Water containers
1″ polyfoam sponge brush
Scruffy old toothbrush *or* stencil brush
Brushes: #6 *or* #8 flat; #1 round

Pencil *or* marking pen
Graphite paper
Tracing paper
Drafting tape
Stylus
Eraser
Wood glue *or* glue gun
Steel wool
Varnish

PALETTE

Delta Ceramcoat	*Jo Sonja Chroma*	*Illinois Bronze*
Light Chocolate	Fawn	★
Jubilee Green	Brilliant Green	Holiday Green
White	Titanium White	Soft White
Cape Cod + White	French Blue + Tintanium White	Light Stoneware Blue
Black	Carbon Black	Soft Black
★	★	Apache Red
Mendocino	Burgundy	Bordeaux
Empire Gold	Turner's Yellow	Dijon Gold

DIRECTIONS

To prepare for this project, please read and follow the General Instructions and Basic Procedures for all projects (beginning on page 200) and the instructions for those particular Special Techniques used in this project (beginning on page 206).

Transfer and Paint the House

1. Paint the house and the dowels in Soft White.
2. Transfer roof, chimneys, windows, door, and striping to the house.
3. Paint roof, chimneys, and windows in Light Stoneware Blue.
4. Paint door and striping in Light Chocolate.
5. Paint fence in Soft Black.

Decorate the House

1. Transfer rose and leaf designs to house.
2. Paint roses in Apache Red.
3. Shade roses in Bordeaux.
4. Mix 1 part Apache Red and 1 part Soft White and use mixture to paint petal design on roses.
5. Paint lined leaves in Soft Black.
6. Mix 2 parts Light Chocolate and 2 parts Holiday Green and use mixture to paint tendrils and remaining leaves.
7. Using Soft Black, paint veins in the green leaves.
8. Add dots in Dijon Gold to center of roses.
9. Using Dijon Gold and the mixtures prepared in steps 4 and 6 above, paint random dots on the floral design.

Complete the Finishing Touches

1. Glue the fence into place.
2. Spatter the bookends in Light Chocolate.
3. Spatter the bookends using the mixture from step 5 of "Decorate the House."
4. Finish with 2 thin coats of varnish.

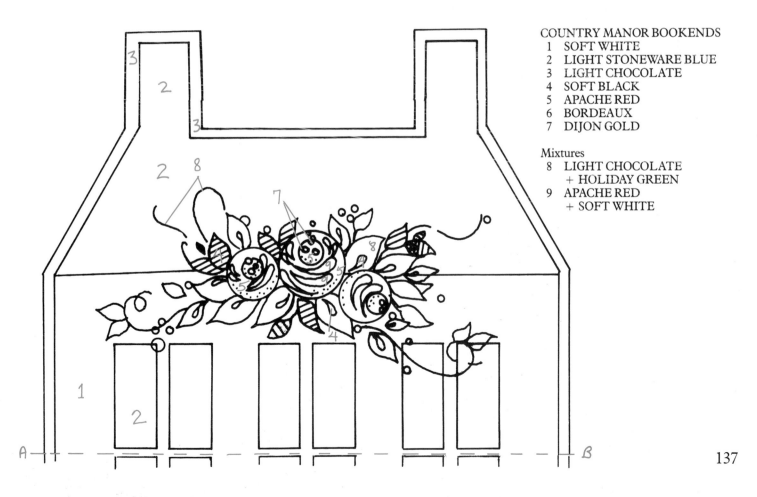

COUNTRY MANOR BOOKENDS
1 SOFT WHITE
2 LIGHT STONEWARE BLUE
3 LIGHT CHOCOLATE
4 SOFT BLACK
5 APACHE RED
6 BORDEAUX
7 DIJON GOLD

Mixtures
8 LIGHT CHOCOLATE
   + HOLIDAY GREEN
9 APACHE RED
   + SOFT WHITE

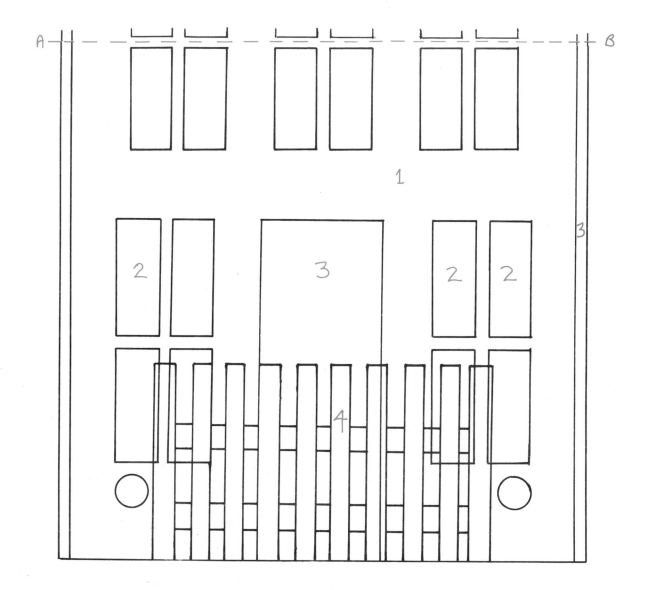

Country Children's Treasures

Bremen Towne Mini Quilt Rack

*While rummaging through musty boxes at an
old gentleman's estate auction, I uncovered
a small, exquisitely handcrafted quilt rack.
I brought it back to the shop and reproduced it,
then added sweet musicians from a favorite story.*

MATERIALS

Wooden mini quilt rack
Sandpaper
Tack cloth
Sealer
Paper towels
Acrylic palette pad
Palette knife
Water containers
1″ polyfoam sponge brush
Brushes: #1 round; #3 round; #8 *or* #10 flat

Pencil *or* marking pen
Graphite paper
Tracing paper
Drafting tape
Stylus
Eraser
Steel wool
Varnish

PALETTE

Delta Ceramcoat	*Jo Sonja Chroma*	*Illinois Bronze*
Antique White	Warm White	Antique White
Bright Red	Napthol Red Light	Jo Sonja Red
Pigskin	★	★
Black	Carbon Black	Soft Black
Raw Sienna	Raw Sienna	Tumbleweed
White	Titanium White	White Wash
Pumpkin	★	True Orange

DIRECTIONS

To prepare for this project, please read and follow the General Instructions and Basic Procedures for all projects (beginning on page 200) and the instructions for those particular Special Techniques used in this project (beginning on page 206).

Paint General Outlines of the Designs

1. Paint quilt rack in Antique White.
2. Transfer general outlines of animals, banners (except lettering), and rack feet to each end of rack. (You may opt to paint only one end.)
3. Paint cows and roosters in White Wash.
4. Mix 4 parts White Wash, ⅛ part Jo Sonja Red, and ⅛ part Pigskin and use mixture to paint pigs. (Save this mixture to use later in the project.)
5. Mix 4 parts White Wash and ⅛ part Soft Black and use mixture to paint sheep.
6. Mix 5 parts Jo Sonja Red and ¾ part Tumbleweed and use mixture to paint top and bottom banners. (Save this mixture to use later in the project.)
7. Shade top and bottom of banners and around animals in Tumbleweed.
8. Using mixture from step 6 above, paint bands on edges of the stand and around the feet of the stand.

Paint the Decorative Details

1. Transfer details of animals and lettering to each end of rack.
2. Using mixture from step 6 of "Paint General Outlines of the Designs," paint the roosters' combs, wattles, wings, and tail feathers.
3. Paint roosters' beaks and feet in one coat of Pigskin.
4. Paint roosters' beaks and feet in one coat of True Orange.
5. Paint roosters' eyes in Soft Black.
6. Shade roosters in Tumbleweed.
7. Mix 1 part Soft Black and ⅛ part Tumbleweed and use mixture to paint sheeps' eyes, noses, feet, and mouth lines.
8. Mix 1 part Soft Black and 1 part Tumbleweed and use mixture to paint sheeps' ears.
9. Using mixture from step 8 above, shade sheep.
10. Paint pigs' eyes in Soft Black.
11. Shade pigs in Tumbleweed.
12. Mix 1 part Soft Black and ⅙ part Tumbleweed and use mixture to paint cows' feet, tails, and markings.
13. Using mixture from step 4 of "Paint General Outlines of the Designs," paint cows' noses and udders. While still damp, add 3 strokes of White Wash to each udder to create teats.
14. Shade udders in Jo Sonja Red.
15. Mix 1 part Soft Black and 1 part Tumbleweed with enough water to thin to a consistency of whipping cream and then use to outline each animal in a broken, trembly line to create a soft border. (Don't worry if your hand is shaky—a shaky line will give a softer effect.)
16. Using mixture from step 6 of "Paint the General Outlines of the Designs," paint hearts on all of the animals.
17. Using the same mixture, paint heart hangers on all of the animals.
18. Paint lettering in Antique White.

Complete the Finishing Touches

1. Finish with 2 thin coats of varnish.

BREMEN TOWNE MINI QUILT RACK
1 ANTIQUE WHITE
2 WHITE WASH
3 PIGSKIN
4 SOFT BLACK
5 TUMBLEWEED
6 JO SONJA RED
7 TRUE ORANGE

Mixtures
8 WHITE WASH
   + JO SONJA RED + PIGSKIN
9 WHITE WASH
   + SOFT BLACK
10 JO SONJA RED
   + TUMBLEWEED
11 SOFT BLACK
   + TUMBLEWEED

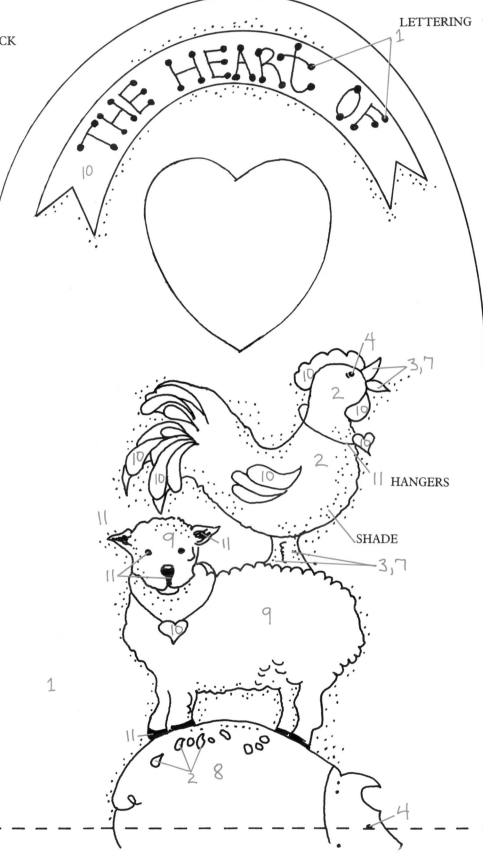

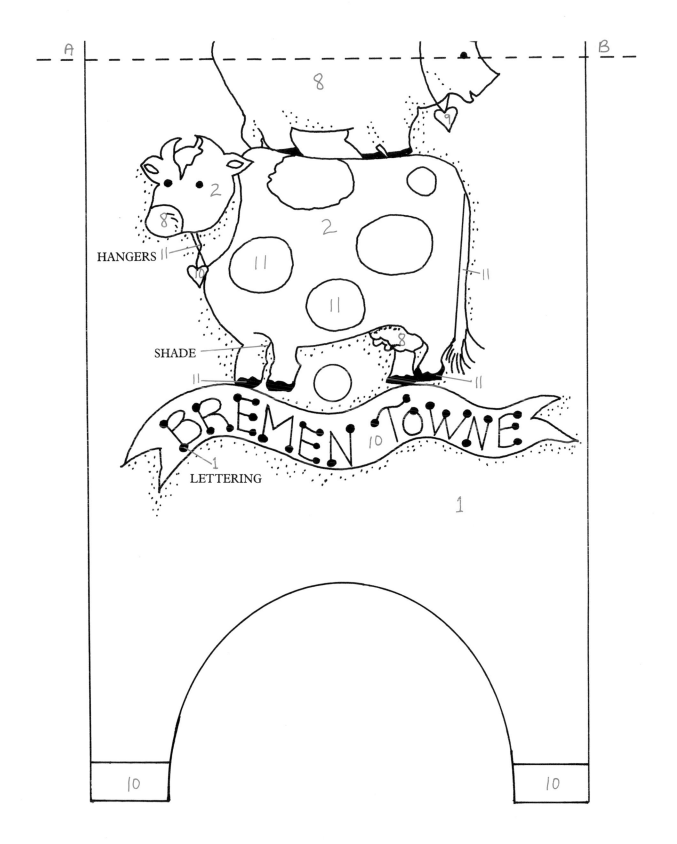

A   B

HANGERS

SHADE

BREMEN TOWNE

LETTERING

Reading Bear Bookends

Here's a quick, easy, and practical project to paint for your own child or as a gift for a new baby. The bright colors and "reader-friendly" brown bears will help impart the subtle yet valuable message that "Reading is fun."

MATERIALS

Wooden bookends kit
Sandpaper
Tack cloth
Sealer
Paper towels
Acrylic palette pad
Palette knife
Water containers
1″ polyfoam sponge brush
Fine-point permanent black marking pen (optional for lettering on small books)
Brushes: #1 round; #3 round; #10 *or* #12 flat

Pencil *or* marking pen
Graphite paper
Tracing paper
Drafting tape
Stylus
Eraser
Wood glue *or* glue gun
Phillips screwdriver
Steel wool
Varnish

PALETTE

Delta Ceramcoat	*Jo Sonja Chroma*	*Illinois Bronze*
★	Colonial Blue + White	Soft Blue
Raw Sienna	Raw Sienna	Tumbleweed
Burnt Umber	Brown Earth	Burnt Umber
Black	Carbon Black	Soft Black
White	★	Soft White
★	★	Purple Canyon
Coral	★	Coral Belles
Straw	Yellow Oxide + Titanium White	Golden Harvest
Bright Red	Napthol Red Light	Jo Sonja Red

DIRECTIONS

To prepare for this project, please read and follow the General Instructions and Basic Procedures for all projects (beginning on page 200) and the instructions for those particular Special Techniques used in this project (beginning on page 206).

Paint the Bears

1. Transfer outlines of head, shirt, and overalls.
2. Paint face, ear, and hand in Tumbleweed.
3. Shade face, ear, and hand in Burnt Umber.
4. Paint nose, mouth line, line of inner ear, eyelash, and iris of eye in Burnt Umber.
5. Paint shoes and pupil in Soft Black.
6. Outline iris in Soft Black.
7. Add twinkle dot to eye in Soft White.
8. Using Floated Color technique, paint cheeks in Jo Sonja Red.
9. Add little whisker dots to snout area in Burnt Umber. (I realize that I'm taking liberties with this detail.)
10. Paint socks and shirt in Purple Canyon.
11. Mix 4 parts Soft Blue and 4 parts White Wash and use mixture to paint overalls. (Save this mixture to use later in the project.)
12. Mix ¾ part Soft Blue and ¼ part Purple Canyon and use mixture to shade overalls. (Save this mixture to use later in the project.)
13. Shade socks in Soft Black.

Transfer and Paint Clothing Details

1. Transfer details to bears.
2. Paint patches on overalls in Purple Canyon.
3. Apply linework to patches in White Wash.
4. Add dots to patches in Golden Harvest.
5. Paint stripes on socks in Coral Belles.
6. Paint roses on shirt in Coral Belles (one coat only).
7. Mix 1 part Soft Blue and 1 part Golden Harvest and use mixture to paint leaves and stems on bear's shirt.
8. Add center dots to roses in Golden Harvest.

9. Paint hanky in White Wash.
10. Using mixture from step 12 of "Paint the Bears," shade the hanky.

Paint and Letter the Base Books

1. Mix 6 parts Soft Blue, 1 part Purple Canyon, and ⅛ part Soft Black and use mixture to paint bases.
2. Paint pages of book bases in White Wash.
3. Transfer lettering to bases.
4. Paint lettering in Soft Black.

Paint and Letter Hand-Held Books and Accessory Books

1. Paint hand-held books in Golden Harvest.
2. Paint hand-held book pages in Soft White.
3. Paint the pages of the small accessory books in Soft White.
4. Paint one book cover in Purple Canyon.
5. Paint one book cover, using the mixture from step 11 of "Paint the Bears."
6. Paint one book cover in Tumbleweed.
7. Paint one book cover in Coral Belles.
8. Paint one book cover in Golden Harvest.
9. Paint one book cover in Soft Blue.
10. Paint one book cover in Burnt Umber.
11. Transfer lettering to hand-held and accessory books (or make up your own titles, if you prefer).
12. Paint lettering in Soft Black or use black marking pen.

Complete the Finishing Touches

1. Assemble bears and small books onto bases. The bears are screwed on from the bottom and the small books are glued on. (Refer to photo.)
2. Finish with 2 thin coats of varnish.

The Book of Bears

READING BEAR BOOKENDS
1 TUMBLEWEED
2 BURNT UMBER
3 PURPLE CANYON
4 WHITE WASH
5 SOFT BLACK
6 GOLDEN HARVEST
7 CORAL BELLES
8 JO SONJA RED

Mixtures
9 SOFT BLUE + WHITE WASH
10 SOFT BLUE + GOLDEN HARVEST

HONEY FACTS
THE BEARS
TWO BEARS
BEAR LIFE
BEAR ALL
BABY BEAR
BEAR FACTS
BOOK of BEARS

Humpty Dumpty Coin Bank

Humpty Dumpty, the well-loved nursery rhyme character, has been transformed into a whimsical bank. Everyone needs a little cache! Paint this for a new baby, a coin bank collector, or even a bank employee if you happen to know one. Don't forget to drop a quarter in the slot to open the account.

MATERIALS

Wooden Humpty Dumpty bank
Sandpaper
Tack cloth
Sealer
Paper towels
Acrylic palette pad
Palette knife
Water containers
Antiquing mud (4-oz. jar) *or* Burnt Umber oil paint
Linseed oil/mineral spirits
Brushes: #8 *or* #10 flat, #1 *or* #3 round

Pencil *or* marking pen
Graphite paper
Tracing paper
Drafting tape
Stylus
Eraser
Wood glue
Steel wool
Varnish

PALETTE

Delta Ceramcoat	*Jo Sonja Chroma*	*Illinois Bronze*
Raw Sienna	Raw Sienna	Tumbleweed
Antique Gold	★	★
Liberty Blue	★	★
Jubilee Green	Brilliant Green	Holiday Green
White	Titanium White	White Wash
Black	Carbon Black	Soft Black
Bright Red	Napthol Red Light	Jo Sonja Red
Trail	Fawn + White	Wicker

DIRECTIONS

To prepare for this project, please read and follow the General Instructions and Basic Procedures for all projects (beginning on page 200) and the instructions for those particular Special Techniques used in this project (beginning on page 206).

Paint Humpty Dumpty

1. Transfer Humpty Dumpty pattern to piece.
2. Paint face and hands in White Wash.
3. Shade face and hands in Tumbleweed.
4. Using Floated Color technique, paint cheeks and tip of nose in Jo Sonja Red. He's got a robust face, so don't be shy about creating a blush.
5. Mix 1 part Liberty Blue and ⅛ part White Wash and use mixture to paint irises of eyes.
6. Outline irises in Liberty Blue.
7. Paint pupils in Soft Black.
8. Add twinkle dot to each eye in White Wash.
9. Mix ¼ part Tumbleweed and ¼ part Soft Black and use mixture to paint eyebrows.
10. Shade under eyebrows in Tumbleweed.
11. Outline chin and nose in Tumbleweed.
12. Shade chin and nose in Tumbleweed.
13. Paint lips in Jo Sonja Red.
14. Paint line from lips to cheeks in Tumbleweed.
15. Shade under this line in Tumbleweed.
16. Add a Soft Black dot to center of lips.

Paint Humpty Dumpty's Clothes

1. Paint jacket in Liberty Blue.
2. Shade jacket in Soft Black.
3. Apply Cross-hatching to sleeves in White Wash.
4. Paint shoes and belt in Soft Black.
5. Paint belt buckle and buttons in Antique Gold.
6. Paint collar and band on sleeve in White Wash.
7. Mix 2 parts Jo Sonja Red and ¾ parts Liberty Blue and use mixture to paint trousers and hat.

8. Crosshatch trousers in Jo Sonja Red.
9. Paint socks and narrow line on hat in White Wash.
10. Add stripes to socks in Liberty Blue.
11. Paint belt buckle and buttons in Antique Gold a second time.

Paint Wall

1. Paint wall in Wicker.
2. Paint ledge in Tumbleweed.
3. Transfer stone wall patterns to all 4 sides.
4. Using Triple-Loaded Color technique and Tumbleweed, Liberty Blue, and Antique Gold, paint approximately one third of the stones, randomly selected.
5. Using Triple-Loaded Color technique and Tumbleweed, Jo Sonja Red, and Soft Black, paint another randomly selected one third of the stones.
6. Using Triple-Loaded Color technique and Tumbleweed, White Wash, and Soft Black, paint remaining one third of stones.
7. Mix ½ part Soft Black and ¼ part Tumbleweed and use mixture to shade a few randomly selected stones.
8. Using Double-Loaded Color technique, paint grass in Jubilee Green and Antique Gold.
9. Highlight grass in White Wash.

Complete the Finishing Touches

1. Glue on arms, legs, and hat.
2. Apply antiquing mud. Allow to dry completely, at least 24 hours.
3. Using Outline-and-Paint technique, highlight collar, bands on sleeve, socks, and hat band in White Wash.
4. Using Outline-and-Paint technique, highlight grass in Antique Gold.
5. Using Outline-and-Paint technique, highlight trousers and hat in Jo Sonja Red.
6. Finish with 2 thin coats of varnish.

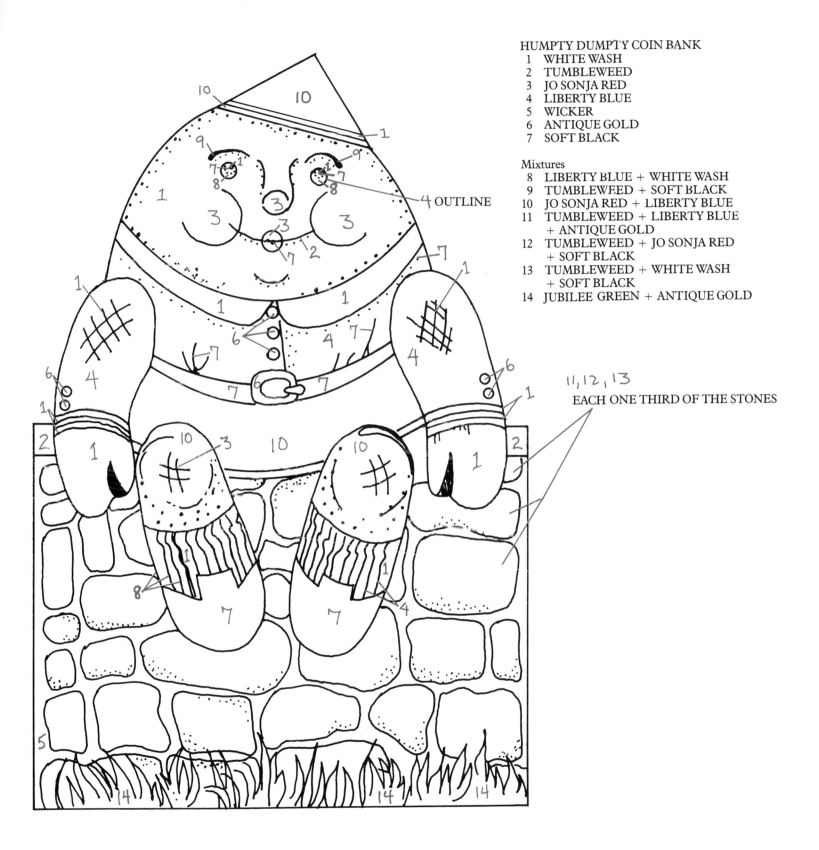

HUMPTY DUMPTY COIN BANK
1 WHITE WASH
2 TUMBLEWEED
3 JO SONJA RED
4 LIBERTY BLUE
5 WICKER
6 ANTIQUE GOLD
7 SOFT BLACK

Mixtures
8 LIBERTY BLUE + WHITE WASH
9 TUMBLEWEED + SOFT BLACK
10 JO SONJA RED + LIBERTY BLUE
11 TUMBLEWEED + LIBERTY BLUE
   + ANTIQUE GOLD
12 TUMBLEWEED + JO SONJA RED
   + SOFT BLACK
13 TUMBLEWEED + WHITE WASH
   + SOFT BLACK
14 JUBILEE GREEN + ANTIQUE GOLD

11,12,13
EACH ONE THIRD OF THE STONES

OUTLINE

151

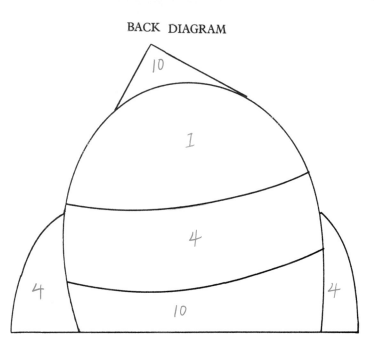

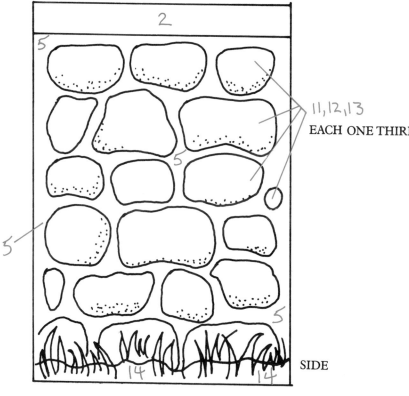

11,12,13

EACH ONE THIRD OF THE STONES

SIDE

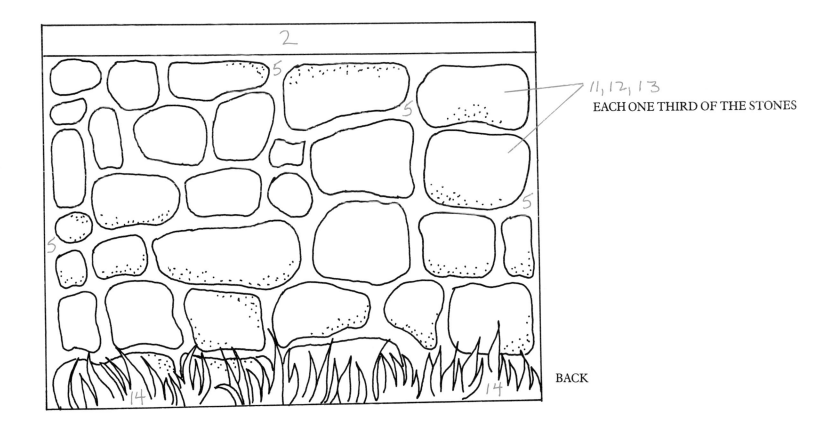

2

5

5

11, 12, 13
EACH ONE THIRD OF THE STONES

5

5

BACK

14

14

153

Noah's Ark Pegboard

This adaptation of the Noah's Ark theme came from a request for a reasonably priced pegboard for a small child. It's charming, and children love identifying the animals while learning to hang things up.

MATERIALS

Wooden Noah's Ark pegboard kit
Sandpaper
Tack cloth
Sealer
Paper towels
Acrylic palette pad
Palette knife
Water containers
1″ polyfoam sponge brush
Brushes: #1 round; #5 round; #8 flat; ¼″ stencil
  brush

Pencil *or* marking pen
Graphite paper
White transfer paper
Tracing paper
Drafting tape
Stylus
Eraser
Wood glue *or* glue gun
Steel wool
Varnish

PALETTE

Delta Ceramcoat	*Jo Sonja Chroma*	*Illinois Bronze*
Boston Fern	★	★
Autumn Brown	Raw Sienna	Tumbleweed
Pigskin	★	★
Bright Red	Napthol Red Light	Jo Sonja Red
Black	Carbon Black	Soft Black
Antique White	Warm White	Antique White
Colonial Blue	Aqua	Marina Blue
Medium Flesh + Antique White	★	Light Peaches n' Cream
Coral	★	Coral Belles
Burnt Umber	Brown Earth	Burnt Umber

DIRECTIONS

To prepare for this project, please read and follow the General Instructions and Basic Procedures for all projects (beginning on page 200) and the instructions for those particular Special Techniques used in this project (beginning on page 206).

Paint the Ark

1. Transfer general outlines of hull and cabin to plaque.
2. Paint hull, mini pegs, dowel, and chimney in Boston Fern.
3. Paint a stripe on top of the chimney in Marina Blue. (Refer to photo.)
4. Mix 5 parts Jo Sonja Red and 1 part Burnt Umber and use mixture to paint roof. (Save this mixture to use later in the project.)
5. Using Floated Color technique, highlight roof in Coral Belles.
6. Mix 2 parts Soft Black and ½ part Burnt Umber and use mixture to paint crow on top of chimney.
7. Paint crow's eye in Marina Blue. (Save this mixture to use later in the project.)
8. Mix 6 parts Tumbleweed and ¼ part Burnt Umber and use mixture to paint cabin. (Save this mixture to use later in the project.)
9. Transfer general outlines of animals and windows.
10. Using mixture from step 6 above, paint windows.

Paint the Animals

1. Paint pig in Coral Belles.
2. Paint cows in Antique White.
3. Using mixture from step 6 of "Paint the Ark," paint markings on cows.
4. Shade cows in Tumbleweed.
5. Paint cows' noses in Coral Belles.
6. Paint giraffes in Pigskin.
7. Using mixture from step 8 of "Paint the Ark," paint giraffes' markings.
8. Using mixture from step 6 of "Paint the Ark," underline bottom sides of markings on giraffes.
9. Shade giraffes with Burnt Umber.
10. Mix ½ part Pigskin and 1¼ part Antique White and use mixture to paint cat. (Save this mixture to use later in the project.)
11. Using mixture from step 6 of "Paint the Ark," paint cat nose and whiskers.
12. Using mixture from step 11 above, paint all of the animals' eyes.

Paint Noah and Banner

1. Paint Noah's face and hands in Light Peaches n' Cream.
2. Using mixture from step 6 of "Paint the Ark," paint Noah's eyes.
3. Paint Noah's mouth in Jo Sonja Red.
4. Using Side-Loaded Color technique, paint Noah's nose in Jo Sonja Red.
5. Using Floated Color technique, paint Noah's cheeks in Coral Belles.
6. Paint Noah's coat in Marina Blue.
7. Using mixture from step 6 of "Paint the Ark," paint Noah's hat and eyebrows.
8. Paint coat buttons in Tumbleweed.
9. Mix 3 parts Burnt Umber and ¼ part Soft Black and use mixture to paint Noah's hair and banner.
10. Using mixture from step 10 of "Paint the Animals," add lettering to banner.

Paint Details and Lettering on Ark

1. Using Triple-Loaded Color technique, paint the water in Marina Blue, Antique White, and Boston Fern. Apply with wavy motion of brush.
2. Using same technique and colors as in step 1 above, paint large rounded strokes above the wavy strokes.
3. Mix 1 part Marina Blue, 1 part Antique White, and ¼ part Boston Fern and use mixture to paint fish.
4. Using mixture from step 3 above, paint lines on hull of ark. (If these lines appear too stark, as mine did, subdue them by using Dry Brush Color technique with Boston Fern.)
5. Add dots to back of fish in Antique White. Use tip of brush to keep dots close together.
6. Add eyes to fish in Soft Black.
7. Using mixture from step 4 of "Paint the Ark," paint the ladybugs.
8. Paint details on ladybugs in Soft Black.
9. Paint flowerpots in Pigskin.
10. Using mixture from step 3 above, use stencil brush and fill in pots.
11. Using mixture from step 4 of "Paint the Ark," randomly add dots to foliage in pots.
12. Add lettering to hull in Soft Black.
13. Using mixture from step 10 of "Paint the Animals," highlight one side of lettering. (Refer to photo.)

Complete the Finishing Touches

1. Glue pegs into pegboard; glue dowel into chimney; glue crow onto dowel.
2. Finish with 2 thin coats of varnish.

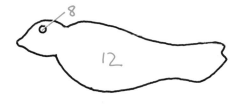

NOAH'S ARK PEGBOARD
1   BOSTON FERN
2   TUMBLEWEED
3   CORAL BELLES
4   ANTIQUE WHITE
5   PIGSKIN
6   LIGHT PEACHES N' CREAM
7   SOFT BLACK
8   MARINA BLUE
9   BURNT UMBER
10 JO SONJA RED

Mixtures
11 JO SONJA RED + BURNT UMBER
12 SOFT BLACK + BURNT UMBER
13 MARINA BLUE + ANTIQUE WHITE + BOSTON FERN
14 PIGSKIN + ANTIQUE WHITE
15 ANTIQUE WHITE + JO SONJA RED
16 TUMBLEWEED + BURNT UMBER

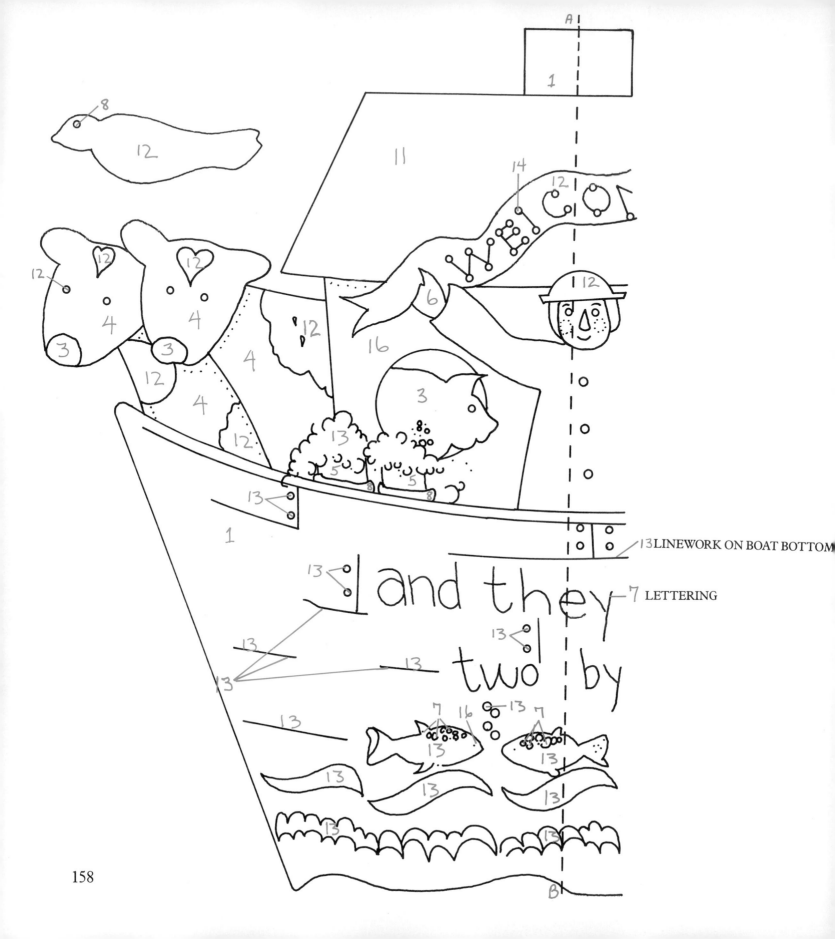

13 LINEWORK ON BOAT BOTTOM

7 LETTERING

158

159

Noah's Ark Mirror

When I first saw these little animals, I thought I might turn them into my favorite accessory, a necklace. When they were finished, however, I decided I'd like them better on a child's or family room piece, so I added them to the mirror to be seen and enjoyed all of the time. Shown, page 155.

MATERIALS

Wooden frame and figures; mirror
Sandpaper
Tack cloth
Sealer
Paper towels
Acrylic palette pad
Palette knife
Water containers
1″ polyfoam sponge brush
Antiquing mud (4-oz. jar) *or* Burnt Umber oil paint
Linseed oil/mineral spirits
Faux finish combing tool
Retarder
Brushes: #1 round; #4 flat

Pencil *or* marking pen
White transfer paper
Tracing paper
Drafting tape
Stylus
Eraser
Wood glue *or* glue gun
Steel wool
Varnish

PALETTE

Delta Ceramcoat	*Jo Sonja Chroma*	*Illinois Bronze*
Black	Carbon Black	Soft Black
Burnt Umber	Brown Earth	Burnt Umber
Mendocino	Burgundy	Bordeaux
Medium Flesh + White	Opal	Light Peaches n' Cream
Raw Sienna	Raw Sienna	Tumbleweed
Cadet Grey	Nimbus Grey	Soft Grey
Burnt Sienna	Burnt Sienna	Burnt Sienna
Pigskin	★	★
Boston Fern	★	★

DIRECTIONS

To prepare for this project, please read and follow the General Instructions and Basic Procedures for all projects (beginning on page 200) and the instructions for those particular Special Techniques used in this project (beginning on page 206).

Paint the Frame

1. Paint frame in Pigskin.
2. Sand frame lightly to smooth finish.
3. Mix 10 parts Burnt Umber and 2 parts Retarder and apply this mixture in liberal amounts to the face of the frame.
4. Apply squiggly pattern to the frame with combing tool. Set aside and allow to dry completely before handling.
5. Paint edges of frame in Burnt Umber.
6. Paint backside of frame in Burnt Umber. (This will prevent the reflection of bare wood in the mirror.)

Transfer and Paint Noah and Mrs. Noah

1. Transfer general outline to Noah and Mrs. Noah.
2. Paint robe with hood on Mrs. Noah in Bordeaux.
3. Paint robe with hood on Noah in Boston Fern.
4. Paint their faces and hands in Light Peaches n' Cream.
5. Transfer details of hands and faces to Noah and Mrs. Noah.
6. Mix ⅛ part Tumbleweed and ⅛ part Soft Grey and use mixture to paint Noah's beard.
7. Paint Mrs. Noah's hair in Tumbleweed.
8. Paint their eyes in Soft Black.
9. Mix ¼ part Light Peaches n' Cream and ¼ part Bordeaux and use mixture to paint her cheeks and his nose.
10. Paint their mouths in Bordeaux.

Transfer and Paint the Ark

1. Transfer general outline to ark.
2. Paint the hull of the ark in Boston Fern.
3. Paint the cabin in Bordeaux.
4. Mix 2 parts Tumbleweed and 2 parts Soft Grey and use mixture to paint the roof and the door. (Save this mixture to use later in the project.)

Paint the Animals

1. Using mixture from step 4 of "Transfer and Paint the Ark," paint the elephants.
2. Paint donkeys in Burnt Sienna.
3. Paint camels in Burnt Umber.
4. Paint lions and giraffes in Pigskin.
5. Transfer details to animals.
6. Paint elephant tail, eyes, and feet in Soft Black.
7. Shade elephants in Soft Black.
8. Paint donkey tails, eyes, hoofs, and noses in Soft Black.
9. Shade donkeys in Burnt Umber.
10. Paint camel tails, eyes, hoofs, and noses in Soft Black.
11. Shade camels in Soft Black.
12. Paint lion eyes, noses, and mouths in Soft Black.
13. Paint lion paws in Burnt Umber.
14. Paint lion tails and manes in Burnt Sienna.
15. Paint giraffe tails, hoofs, and markings in Burnt Sienna.
16. Paint giraffe eyes in Soft Black.
17. Paint giraffe noses in Burnt Umber.

Complete the Finishing Touches

1. Apply antiquing mud to Noah and all figures, taking care not to antique their backsides. Allow to dry completely, at least 24 hours.
2. Glue pieces onto frame.
3. Finish with 2 thin coats of varnish.
4. Install mirror.

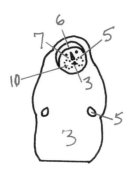

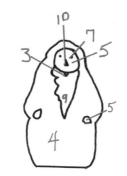

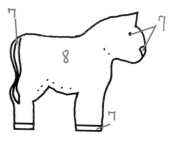

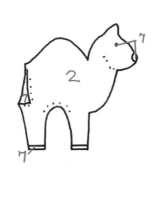

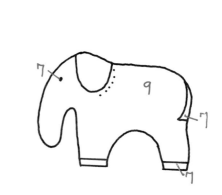

NOAH'S ARK MIRROR
1 PIGSKIN
2 BURNT UMBER
3 BORDEAUX
4 BOSTON FERN
5 LIGHT PEACHES N' CREAM
6 TUMBLEWEED
7 SOFT BLACK
8 BURNT SIENNA

Mixtures
9 TUMBLEWEED + SOFT GREY
10 LIGHT PEACHES N' CREAM + BORDEAUX

Noah's Ark Set

*Early settlers handcrafted Noah and the ark for their children's
Sunday playtime, to amuse them while keeping the Sabbath.
Artistic liberties have been taken here in reducing
the number of on-board critters, but the essence and spirit
of Noah remain to charm children of all ages.*

MATERIALS

Wooden Noah's Ark kit
Sandpaper
Tack cloth
Sealer
Paper towels
Acrylic palette pad
Palette knife
Water containers
1″ polyfoam sponge brush
Antiquing mud (4-oz. jar) *or* Burnt Umber oil paint
Linseed oil/mineral spirits
Scruffy old toothbrush *or* stencil brush
Brushes: #2 flat; #8 *or* #10 flat; #3 round

Pencil *or* marking pen
White transfer paper
Tracing paper
Drafting tape
Stylus
Eraser
Steel wool
Varnish

PALETTE

Delta Ceramcoat	Jo Sonja Chroma	Illinois Bronze
Medium Flesh	Opal	Light Peaches n' Cream
Straw	Yellow Oxide + White	Golden Harvest
★	★	Apache Red
Cadet Grey	Nimbus Grey	Soft Grey
Antique White	★	Antique White
Raw Sienna	Raw Sienna	Tumbleweed
Mendocino	Burgundy	Bordeaux
Burnt Sienna	Burnt Sienna	Burnt Sienna
Burnt Umber	Brown Earth	Burnt Umber
Boston Fern	★	★
★	★	Light Coral Belles
Pumpkin	★	True Orange
Pigskin	★	★
Black	Carbon Black	Soft Black

DIRECTIONS

To prepare for this project, please read and follow the General Instructions and Basic Procedures for all projects (beginning on page 200) and the instructions for those particular Special Techniques used in this project (beginning on page 206).

Paint the Ark and Figures

1. Using Distressing technique, lightly distress the figures and the ark.
2. Mix 6 parts Golden Harvest and ½ part Boston Fern and use mixture to paint roof of ark.
3. Paint cabin in Bordeaux.
4. Paint hull and ramp in Boston Fern.
5. Paint dove, chickens, and cows in Antique White.
6. Mix 2 parts Antique White and 2 parts Soft Grey and use mixture to paint sheep and elephants. (Save this mixture to use later in the project.)
7. Paint giraffes and lions in Pigskin.
8. Mix 3 parts Burnt Umber and ½ part Burnt Sienna and use mixture to paint hippos.
9. Paint pigs in Light Coral Belles.
10. Mix 2 parts Tumbleweed and 2 parts Soft Grey and use mixture to paint rabbits.

Paint Details of Noah and Mrs. Noah

1. Transfer general outlines to Noah and Mrs. Noah.
2. Paint faces and hands in Peaches n' Cream.
3. Paint Noah's robe in Bordeaux.
4. Paint Mrs. Noah's robe in Boston Fern.
5. Transfer details to Noah and Mrs. Noah.
6. Paint eyes in Soft Black.
7. Using Side-Loaded Color technique and #2 flat brush, paint noses in Apache Red.
8. Using Floated Color technique, paint cheeks in Apache Red.
9. Mix 1 part Apache Red and ½ part Bordeaux and use mixture to paint lips.
10. Using mixture from step 6 of "Paint the Ark and Figures," paint Noah's hair, beard, mustache, and eyebrows.
11. Shade under Noah's beard in Soft Black.
12. Paint Mrs. Noah's hair and eyebrows in Tumbleweed.
13. Paint wide collar and band on Mrs. Noah's robe in Bordeaux.
14. Paint piping on Mrs. Noah's robe in Golden Harvest.

Paint Details of Animals

1. Transfer details to the animals.
2. Paint the eyes on all the animals in Soft Black.
3. Paint dove's beak in True Orange.
4. Shade dove in Burnt Sienna.
5. Paint chickens' beaks and feet in True Orange.
6. Paint the cows' ears, hoofs, tails, and markings in Soft Black.
7. Paint cows' udders and noses in Light Coral Belles.
8. Mix 1 part Soft Black and 1 part Burnt Umber and use mixture to shade cows.
9. Paint sheep's noses, mouths, feet, and legs in Soft Black.
10. Using mixture from step 8 above, shade sheep.
11. Paint elephants' tails and feet in Soft Black.
12. Using mixture from step 8 above, shade elephants.
13. Paint giraffes' noses and hoofs in Soft Black.
14. Paint giraffes' markings in Burnt Umber.
15. Paint hippos' noses and feet in Soft Black.
16. Shade hippos in Soft Black.
17. Add twinkle dots to hippos' eyes in Tumbleweed.
18. Paint pigs' hoofs in Soft Black.
19. Using Floated Color technique, paint pigs' markings in Tumbleweed.
20. Shade pigs in Burnt Umber.

21. Paint rabbits' noses in Soft Black.
22. Paint rabbits' tails in Antique White.
23. Shade rabbits in Burnt Sienna.
24. Paint lions' noses and mouth lines in Soft Black.
25. Paint lions' tails, manes, and claws in True Orange.

Paint and Letter the Bible

1. Paint Bible cover in Soft Black.
2. Paint Bible pages in Antique White.
3. Paint lettering in Golden Harvest.

Paint Details of Ark

1. Transfer details to cabin.
2. Paint windows on cabin in Boston Fern.
3. Paint cabin door in Golden Harvest.

Complete the Finishing Touches

1. Use sandpaper to age all the pieces.
2. Apply antiquing mud. Allow to dry completely, at least 24 hours.
3. Using Outline-and-Paint technique, highlight all pieces.
4. Apply spattering to all pieces—first in Soft Black and then in Boston Fern.
5. Finish with 2 thin coats of varnish.

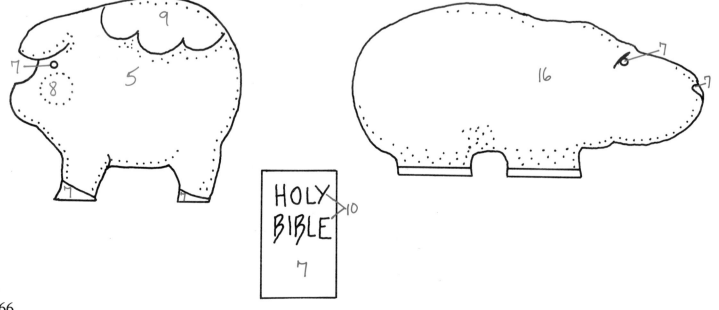

NOAH'S ARK SET
1 BORDEAUX
2 BOSTON FERN
3 ANTIQUE WHITE
4 PIGSKIN
5 LIGHT CORAL BELLES
6 LIGHT PEACHES N' CREAM
7 SOFT BLACK
8 APACHE RED
9 TUMBLEWEED
10 GOLDEN HARVEST
11 TRUE ORANGE
12 BURNT SIENNA
13 BURNT UMBER

Mixtures
14 GOLDEN HARVEST + BOSTON FERN
15 ANTIQUE WHITE + SOFT GREY
16 BURNT UMBER + BURNT SIENNA
17 TUMBLEWEED + SOFT GREY
18 APACHE RED + BORDEAUX
19 SOFT BLACK + BURNT UMBER

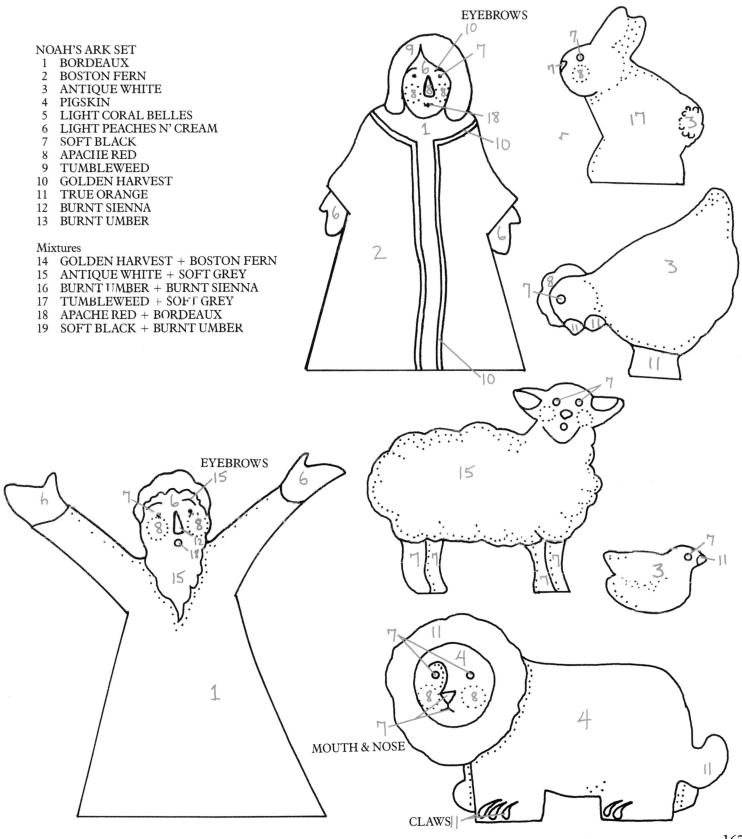

EYEBROWS

EYEBROWS

MOUTH & NOSE

CLAWS

167

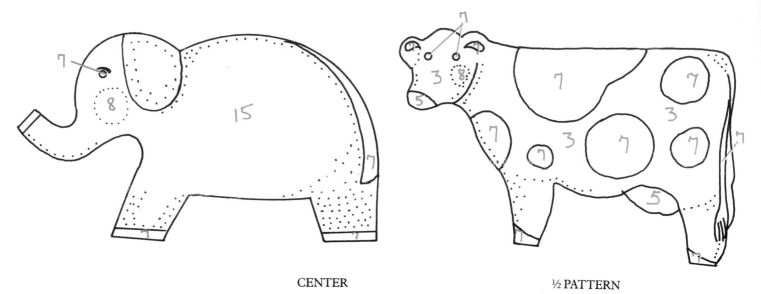

CENTER ½ PATTERN

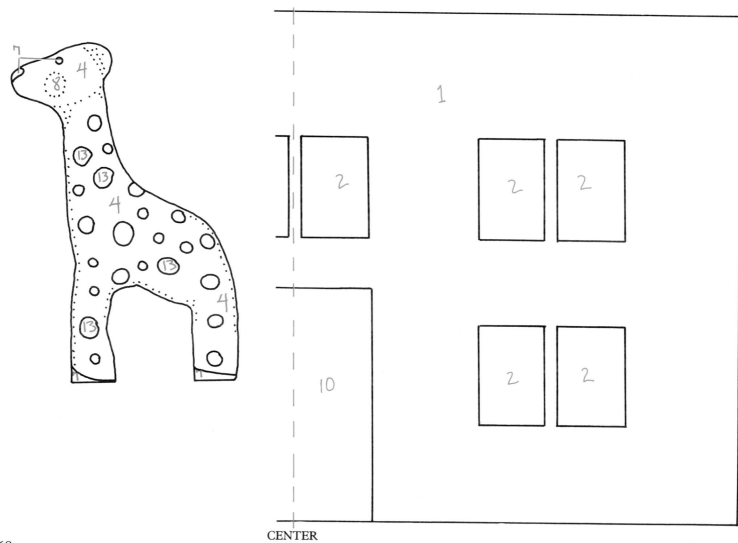

CENTER

Bunny Garden Basket

*This basket was designed to hold a young girl's treasures,
but upon completion, we decided it could also be used
to hold Easter "grass" and muffins (preferably carrot muffins)
for our Easter brunch. After Easter you could
set a container of yellow daffodils or pink geraniums or
impatiens in it, or keep it filled with party-size napkins.*

MATERIALS

Wooden rabbit basket
Sandpaper
Tack cloth
Sealer
Paper towels
Acrylic palette pad
Palette knife
Water containers
1″ polyfoam sponge brush
Brushes: #1 round; #3 round; #10 flat; ¾″–1½″
   glaze brush

Pencil *or* marking pen
Graphite paper
Tracing paper
Drafting tape
Stylus
Eraser
Wood glue *or* glue gun
String *or* crochet thread
Steel wool
Varnish

PALETTE

Delta Ceramcoat	Jo Sonja Chroma	Illinois Bronze
★	★	Light Village Green
Coral + White	★	Light Coral Belles
Antique White	★	Antique White
★	★	Tumbleweed
White	★	Soft White
★	★	L' Orangerie
Bright Yellow	Cadmium Yellow Mid "C"	Sunkiss Yellow
Lilac	★	Wild Hyacinth
Black	Carbon Black	Soft Black

DIRECTIONS

To prepare for this project, please read and follow the General Instructions and Basic Procedures for all projects (beginning on page 200) and the instructions for those particular Special Techniques used in this project (beginning on page 206).

Paint the Fence, Tulips, and Carrots

1. Paint fence, flower stems, and carrot tops in Light Seafoam Green.
2. Paint carrots in L'Orangerie.
3. Paint half of the tulips in Sunkiss Yellow.
4. Paint remaining tulips in Wild Hyacinth.

Transfer and Paint the Rabbits

1. Transfer pattern to rabbit. (Facial details will be transferred later.)
2. Paint rabbit face and ears in Antique White.
3. Shade entire face and ears in Tumbleweed.
4. Transfer facial details.
5. Using Transparent Wash technique, paint inner ear in Tumbleweed.
6. Paint eyes in Soft Black.
7. Outline eyelids, nose, mouth lines, and inner ears in Tumbleweed.
8. Add whisker dots in Tumbleweed.
9. Paint whiskers in Tumbleweed.
10. Using Floated Color technique, paint cheeks in Light Coral Belles.
11. Paint nose in Light Coral Belles.
12. Outline nose again in Tumbleweed.
13. Apply Light Coral Belles on top of Tumbleweed on mouthline.

Paint the Rabbits' Clothing

1. Paint each dress in Light Coral Belles.
2. Paint stockings in Soft White.
3. Transfer linework onto stockings.
4. Paint linework on stockings in Wild Hyacinth.
5. Paint shoes in Tumbleweed.
6. Shade stockings in Tumbleweed.
7. Shade dresses in Tumbleweed.
8. Transfer details onto each dress.
9. Following curling lines carefully, paint flowers on dresses in Sunkiss Yellow.
10. Paint leaves on dresses in Light Village Green.

Complete the Finishing Touches

1. Glue tulips and rabbits in place. (Refer to photo.)
2. Finish with 2 thin coats of varnish.
3. Add carrots around necks with crochet thread or string.

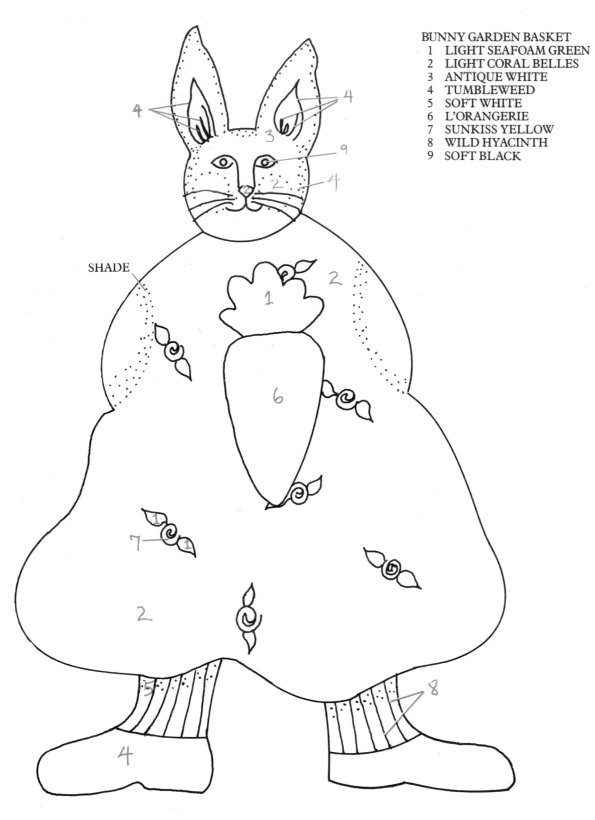

BUNNY GARDEN BASKET
1   LIGHT SEAFOAM GREEN
2   LIGHT CORAL BELLES
3   ANTIQUE WHITE
4   TUMBLEWEED
5   SOFT WHITE
6   L'ORANGERIE
7   SUNKISS YELLOW
8   WILD HYACINTH
9   SOFT BLACK

SHADE

7 OR 8

Country Christmas

Wintry Snowmen Centerpiece Set

These irresistible little snowmen will add just the right amount of holiday spirit to your table or mantel. Embellished with cloves, they have a delicious scent, too. Change the candles from red to whatever color fits your decor.

MATERIALS

Wooden snowmen centerpiece kit
Sandpaper
Tack cloth
Sealer
Whole cloves
Small twigs
Greenery and berries (optional)
Candles (optional)
Scarf material (optional)
Metal candle cups *or* aluminum foil
Antiquing mud (4-oz. jar) *or* Burnt Umber oil paint
Linseed oil/mineral spirits
Brushes: #8 *or* #10 flat; ¼″ stencil brush

Paper towels
Acrylic palette pad
Palette knife
Pencil *or* marking pen
Water containers
Graphite paper
Tracing paper
Stylus
Eraser
Ruler
Wood glue *or* glue gun
Steel wool
Varnish

PALETTE

Delta Ceramcoat	*Jo Sonja Chroma*	*Illinois Bronze*
White	Titanium White	White Wash
Black	Carbon Black	Soft Black
Bright Red	Napthol Red Light	Jo Sonja Red
Pumpkin	★	True Orange

DIRECTIONS

To prepare for this project, please read and follow the General Instructions and Basic Procedures for all projects (beginning on page 200) and the instructions for those particular Special Techniques used in this project (beginning on page 206).

Note: Snowmen come with predrilled holes for embellishments.

Paint the Snowmen
1. Paint snowmen in 3 or 4 coats of White Wash.
2. Paint hats in Soft Black.
3. Paint noses in True Orange.
4. Using Dry Brush Color technique, paint cheeks in Jo Sonja Red.

Paint the Blocks
1. Paint blocks in White Wash.
2. Transfer checker pattern to blocks.
3. Paint alternate squares in Soft Black.

Complete the Finishing Touches
1. Apply antiquing mud to blocks and snowmen. Allow to dry completely, at least 24 hours.
2. Glue twig arms and noses to snowmen.
3. Glue cloves as eyes, mouths, and buttons of snowmen.
4. Finish with 2 thin coats of varnish.
5. Add scarves, greenery, berries, and candles, if desired. If using candles, insert metal candle cups or aluminum foil in hats as a safety precaution.

WINTRY SNOWMEN CENTERPIECE SET
1　WHITE WASH
2　SOFT BLACK
3　TRUE ORANGE
4　JO SONJA RED

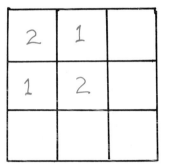

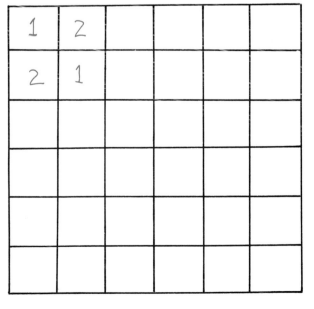

175

Pine Tree Napkin Rings

This simple and easy project proves that "Less is more."
These charming, hand-painted napkin rings are fun
to make and fun to use on your holiday dinner table.
They're also wonderful to give as gifts, to sell at
church bazaars, or to use as scout or class projects.

MATERIALS
Wooden napkin rings
Sandpaper
Tack cloth
Sealer
Paper towels
Acrylic palette pad
Palette knife
Water containers
1" polyfoam sponge brush
Antiquing mud (4-oz. jar) *or* Burnt Umber oil paint
Linseed oil/mineral spirits
Scruffy old toothbrush *or* stencil brush

Stylus
Eraser
Steel wool
Varnish

PALETTE

Delta Ceramcoat	*Jo Sonja Chroma*	*Illinois Bronze*
Woodland Night	★	Prairie Green
Empire Gold	Turner's Yellow	Dijon Gold

DIRECTIONS
To prepare for this project, please read and follow the General Instructions and Basic Procedures for all projects (beginning on page 200) and the instructions for those particular Special Techniques used in this project (beginning on page 206).

Paint the Napkin Rings
1. Paint napkin rings in Prairie Green.
2. Sand openings thoroughly so that they're smooth to the touch.
3. Re-coat napkin rings in Prairie Green if needed.
4. Spatter rings in Dijon Gold.

Complete the Finishing Touches
1. Apply antiquing mud. Allow to dry completely, at least 24 hours.
2. Finish with 3 or 4 coats of varnish.

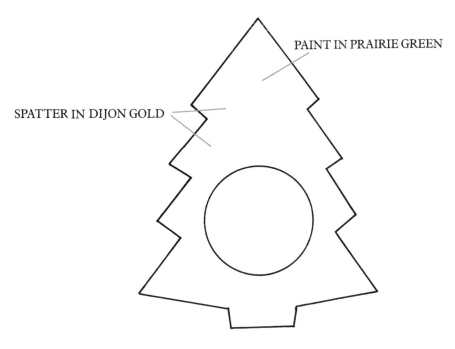

PAINT IN PRAIRIE GREEN

SPATTER IN DIJON GOLD

PINE TREE NAPKIN RINGS
PRAIRIE GREEN
DIJON GOLD

St. Nick's Christmas Card Holder

When we decided to change our Christmas mantel display from Christmas cards to the collection of Santas that I have painted—along with those from friends and family—we needed a new way to display the cards. This basket makes it easy to read and enjoy the cards and keeps them together in one central spot.

MATERIALS

Wooden Santa card holder
Sandpaper
Tack cloth
Sealer
Paper towels
Acrylic palette pad
Palette knife
Water containers
1″ polyfoam sponge brush
Antiquing mud (4-oz. jar) *or* Burnt Umber oil paint
Linseed oil/mineral spirits
Scruffy old toothbrush *or* stencil brush
Brushes: #1 round; #3 round

Pencil *or* marking pen
Graphite paper
White transfer paper
Tracing paper
Drafting tape
Stylus
Eraser
Wood glue (preferred) *or* glue gun
Rubber bands
Steel wool
Varnish

PALETTE

Delta Ceramcoat	Jo Sonja Chroma	Illinois Bronze
Mendocino	Burgundy	Bordeaux
Salem Green	★	Telemark Green
Black	Carbon Black	Soft Black
White	Titanium White	White Wash
Bright Red	Napthol Red Light	Jo Sonja Red
★	★	Peaches n' Cream
Raw Sienna	Raw Sienna	Tumbleweed
Pumpkin	★	True Orange
Cadet Gray	Nimbus Grey	Soft Grey
Empire Gold	Turner's Yellow	Dijon Gold

DIRECTIONS

To prepare for this project, please read and follow the General Instructions and Basic Procedures for all projects (beginning on page 200) and the instructions for those particular Special Techniques used in this project (beginning on page 206).

Transfer and Paint Facial Features

1. Transfer outlines of Santa's hat, hair, face, mustache and beard.
2. Paint face in Peaches n' Cream.
3. Transfer details of face.
4. Paint area behind teeth in Soft Black.
5. Paint teeth in White Wash.
6. Shade teeth in Tumbleweed.
7. Mix ¼ part Jo Sonja Red, ¼ part Bordeaux, and ¼ part Peaches n' Cream and use mixture to paint lips.
8. Shade lips in Bordeaux.
9. Paint nostrils in one coat of Soft Black.
10. Using Tumbleweed and Floated Color technique, create nose. Allow to dry completely and reapply as desired for depth of color.
11. Shade around nostrils in Tumbleweed.
12. Using Tumbleweed and Floated Color technique, create furrows on forehead.
13. Dampen "bulb" of nose and, using Floated Color technique, lightly shade in Jo Sonja Red.
14. Highlight one side of nose in White Wash using Side-Loaded Color technique.
15. Fill in entire eye areas with White Wash.
16. Very lightly shade upper half of white eye areas in Tumbleweed.
17. Transfer and paint irises of eyes in Telemark Green.
18. Transfer and paint pupils in Soft Black.
19. Outline irises in Soft Black.
20. Mix ½ part Telemark Green, ½ part White Wash, and ½ part Dijon Gold and use mixture to add 4 small dots to lower half of each iris.
21. Add twinkle dots to eyes in White Wash.
22. Outline around eyes and eyelids in Tumbleweed.
23. Shade under eyes and above eyelid with Tumbleweed.
24. Lightly dampen cheek areas and shade using Jo Sonja Red and Floated Color technique. Allow to dry completely and reapply as needed for depth of color.
25. Highlight cheeks in White Wash.
26. Paint hair, beard, mustache, and eyebrows in three coats of White Wash.
27. Mix 1 part Soft Grey and 1 part White Wash and use mixture to shade hair, beard, mustache, and eyebrows, using a light touch.
28. Outline nose in Tumbleweed.
29. Shade face in Tumbleweed.

Paint Hat and Details

1. Paint hat in White Wash.
2. Shade hat in Tumbleweed.
3. Transfer details of hat, leaves, berries.
4. Paint leaves on hat in Telemark Green.
5. Paint veins on leaves in Soft Black.
6. Paint berries in Bordeaux.
7. Paint berries in Jo Sonja Red.
8. Dampen berries and highlight one side of each berry in True Orange using Side-Loaded Color technique.
9. Shade leaves in Soft Black.
10. Shade around leaves and berries on hat and under leaves and berries on forehead in Tumbleweed.

Paint and Decorate Santa's Suit

1. Paint suit in Bordeaux.
2. Use loose star included in kit for tracing pattern and transfer randomly onto suit.
3. Mix 2 parts Dijon Gold and ¼ part Tumbleweed and use mixture to paint the stars. Paint only one coat. (Save this mixture to use later in the project.)
4. Mix 1 part Soft Black and 2 parts Bordeaux and use mixture to shade suit under beard areas.

Paint and Assemble the Fence

1. Paint the fence in Telemark Green.
2. Test-fit the fence onto Santa piece and note the spots on which to apply glue. Apply glue, fit together, and use rubber bands to hold the assembly together until the glue dries.

Complete the Finishing Touches

1. Apply antiquing mud, if desired (if not, proceed to step 6). Allow to dry completely, at least 24 hours.
2. Highlight hair, mustache, eyebrows, and beard with wispy strokes of White Wash, if desired. (I find it helpful to imagine actual hair when adding these strokes. Eyebrows call for short strokes; hair requires longer strokes following the shape and contour of the area.)
3. Highlight berry centers in Jo Sonja Red.
4. Highlight any areas that may need brightening after antiquing; use the original colors and a light touch.
5. Using mixture from step 3 of "Paint and Decorate Santa's Suit," spatter entire piece.
6. Attach loose star to tip of hat.
7. Finish with 2 light coats of varnish.

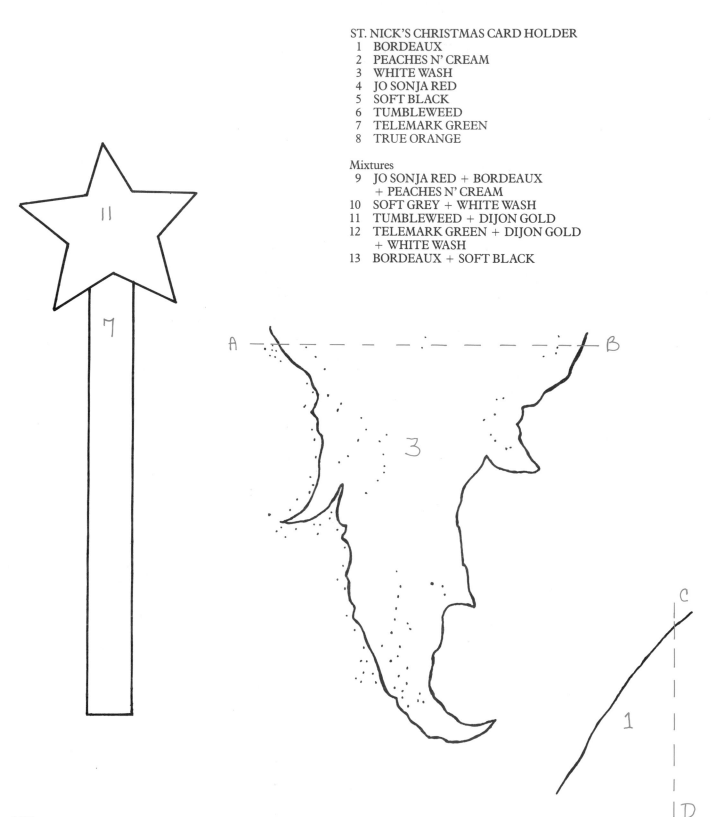

ST. NICK'S CHRISTMAS CARD HOLDER
1   BORDEAUX
2   PEACHES N' CREAM
3   WHITE WASH
4   JO SONJA RED
5   SOFT BLACK
6   TUMBLEWEED
7   TELEMARK GREEN
8   TRUE ORANGE

Mixtures
9   JO SONJA RED + BORDEAUX
    + PEACHES N' CREAM
10 SOFT GREY + WHITE WASH
11 TUMBLEWEED + DIJON GOLD
12 TELEMARK GREEN + DIJON GOLD
    + WHITE WASH
13 BORDEAUX + SOFT BLACK

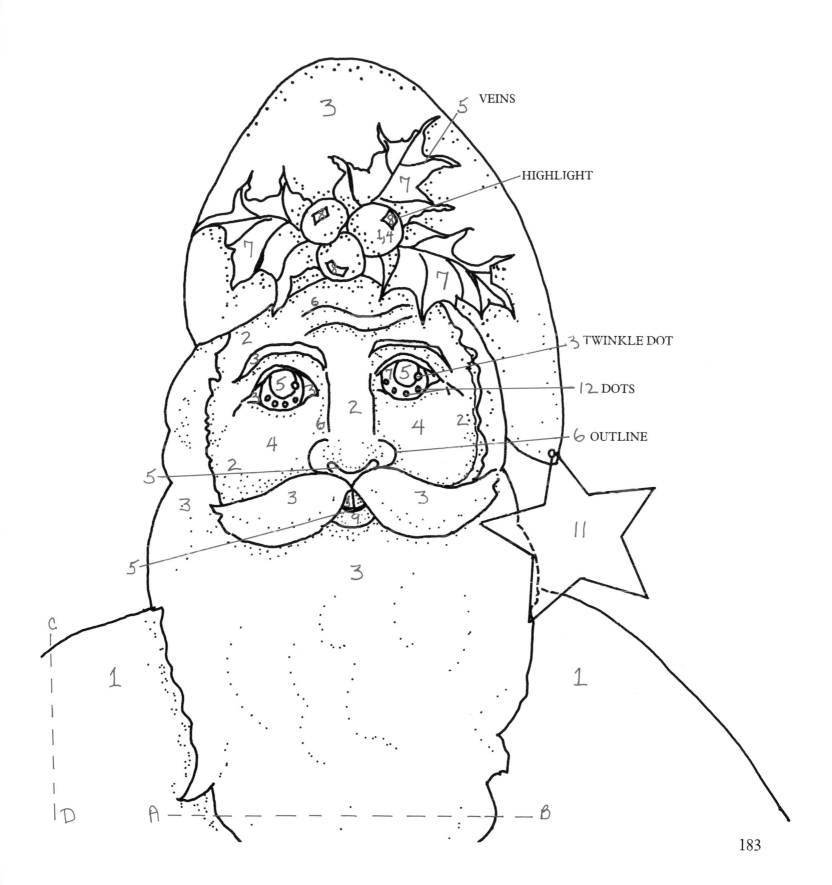

VEINS

HIGHLIGHT

TWINKLE DOT

DOTS

OUTLINE

183

Santa Claus Gift Basket

"Santa Claus is coming to town/be good and kind"
is a gentle admonishment that delivers a timely message.
We've used this basket in a variety of ways—as a centerpiece
with candles and greenery, for serving biscuits or rolls
on a buffet table, and for holding small Christmas presents
for children who drop in.

MATERIALS

Sandpaper
Tack cloth
Sealer
Paper towels
Acrylic palette pad
Palette knife
Water containers
1″ polyfoam sponge brush (2)
Antiquing mud (4-oz. jar) *or* Burnt Umber oil paint
Mineral spirits
Linseed oil
Brushes: #8 *or* #10 flat; #1 *or* #3 round

Pencil *or* marking pen
Graphite paper
Tracing paper
Drafting tape
Stylus
Eraser
Steel wool
Varnish

PALETTE

Delta Ceramcoat	*Jo Sonja Chroma*	*Illinois Bronze*
Raw Sienna	Raw Sienna	Tumbleweed
Woodland Night	★	Prairie Green
Black	Carbon Black	Soft Black
White	Titanium White	Soft White
Bright Red	Napthol Red Light	Jo Sonja Red
★	★	Light Iced Tea
★	★	Light Seafoam Green

DIRECTIONS

To prepare for this project, please read and follow the General Instructions and Basic Procedures for all projects (beginning on page 200) and the instructions for those particular Special Techniques used in this project (beginning on page 206).

Note: The inside and underside of the basket and the sides of each Santa will be stained.

Transfer and Paint General Outlines

1. Transfer general outlines of pattern.
2. Paint green areas including handle in Prairie Green. (Refer to photo.)
3. Paint inset (background of lettering) in Soft White.

Transfer and Paint Facial Details

1. Transfer facial details.
2. Paint faces in Light Iced Tea.
3. Shade faces in Tumbleweed.
4. Using Floated Color technique, paint cheeks in Jo Sonja Red. Repeat as desired for depth of color.
5. Using Floated Color technique, paint tip of nose in Jo Sonja Red.
6. Paint iris of each eye in Tumbleweed.
7. Use stylus to add pupils in Soft Black.
8. Paint eyelashes in Soft Black.
9. Paint twinkle dot on each eye in Soft White.
10. Outline noses in Tumbleweed.
11. Paint hair, beards, mustaches, and eyebrows in Soft White.

Transfer and Paint Coat Details

1. Paint coats and hats in Jo Sonja Red.
2. Transfer details.
3. Mix 1 part Jo Sonja Red and ¼ part Prairie Green and use mixture to create sleeves by shading arms.
4. Paint gloves in Light Seafoam Green.
5. Using mixture from step 3 above, shade around gloves.
6. Paint boots in Soft Black.

Transfer and Paint Lettering and Decorative Details

1. Transfer lettering and holly.
2. Paint lettering in Soft Black.
3. With wooden end of brush, add dots between words and on letters. (Refer to photo and pattern for location and colors of dots.)
4. Paint holly in Prairie Green.
5. Paint berries in Jo Sonja Red.

Complete the Finishing Touches

1. Mix approximately 2 tablespoons of mineral spirits and 2 tablespoons of antiquing solution and apply this mixture, using a rag, to stain the inside and underside of the basket and the sides of each Santa.
2. Apply antiquing mud. Allow to dry completely, at least 24 hours.
3. Using Side-Loaded Color technique, highlight gloves in Light Seafoam Green.
4. Using Side-Loaded Color technique, highlight side of coat and top of hat in Jo Sonja Red.
5. Highlight hair, beards, mustaches, and eyebrows with a few wispy strokes of Soft White.
6. Finish with 2 thin coats of varnish.

SANTA CLAUS GIFT BASKET
1 PRAIRIE GREEN
2 SOFT WHITE
3 SOFT BLACK
4 LIGHT ICED TEA
5 TUMBLEWEED
6 JO SONJA RED
7 LIGHT SEAFOAM GREEN

Mixtures
8 JO SONJA RED + PRAIRIE GREEN

EYE DETAIL

TWINKLE DOT

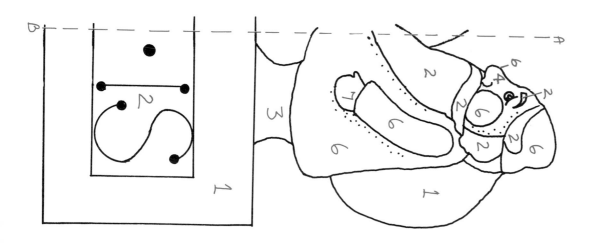

187

Santa and Snowmen Clothespin Tree Trimmers

ἐὰ ἐὰ ἐὰ ἐὰ ἐὰ ἐὰ ἐὰ ἐὰ ἐὰ ἐὰ ἐὰ ἐὰ ἐὰ ἐὰ ἐὰ ἐὰ

*The inspiration for these ornaments came from the shape
of old clothespins, which, when I first saw them,
looked like dolls waiting to be dressed. I couldn't resist
"clothing" them as Santas and snowmen. Slip them over
the branches and they will appear to be standing on the limbs.*

ἐὰ ἐὰ ἐὰ

ἐὰ ἐὰ Santas ἐὰ ἐὰ

MATERIALS

Wood-and-wire clothespin ornament kit (set of 3)
Sandpaper
Tack cloth
Sealer
Paper towels
Acrylic palette pad
Palette knife
Water containers
1″ polyfoam sponge brush
Antiquing mud (4-oz. jar) *or* Burnt Umber oil paint
Linseed oil/mineral spirits
Brushes: #1 *or* #3 round; #8 *or* #10 flat; ¼″ stencil
  brush

Pencil *or* marking pen
Graphite paper
Tracing paper
Drafting tape
Stylus
Eraser
Wood glue *or* glue gun
Steel wool
Varnish

PALETTE

Delta Ceramcoat	*Jo Sonja Chroma*	*Illinois Bronze*
★	★	Light Peaches n' Cream
Bright Red	Napthol Red Light	Jo Sonja Red
Colonial Blue	Aqua	Marina Blue
Woodland Night	★	Prairie Green
★	★	Soft White
Black	Carbon Black	Soft Black
Straw	Yellow Oxide	Golden Harvest

DIRECTIONS

To prepare for this project, please read and follow the General Instructions and Basic Procedures for all projects (beginning on page 200) and the instructions for those particular Special Techniques used in this project (beginning on page 206).

Note: Arms and wire assembly may be removed for easier painting.

SANTA #1

Paint the Santa

1. Transfer general outline of pattern to ornament.
2. Paint face in Light Peaches n' Cream.
3. Paint suit in Jo Sonja Red.
4. Paint heart and boots in Marina Blue.
5. Transfer details to face and heart.
6. Paint hair, beard, mustache, eyebrows, and eyes in Soft White.
7. Add pupils to eyes in Soft Black.
8. Paint mouth in Jo Sonja Red.
9. Using Floated Color technique, paint nose and cheeks in Jo Sonja Red.
10. Add linework to heart in Jo Sonja Red.
11. Add dot to heart in Golden Harvest.
12. Paint ends of arms in Jo Sonja Red.
13. Paint spools in Golden Harvest.
14. Add some random dots to spools in Jo Sonja Red.
15. Add additional random dots to spools in Marina Blue.

Complete the Finishing Touches

1. Glue heart onto Santa.
2. Glue arms and wire assembly into Santa.
3. Apply antiquing mud. Allow to dry completely, at least 24 hours.
4. Lightly sand boots and heart to age.
5. Finish with 2 thin coats of varnish.

SANTA #2

Paint the Santa

1. Transfer general outline of pattern to ornament.
2. Paint face in Light Peaches n' Cream.
3. Paint suit and heart in Jo Sonja Red.
4. Paint boots in Soft Black.
5. Paint stars in Soft White.
6. Paint moon in Golden Harvest.
7. Paint arms in Prairie Green.
8. Paint dots on arms in Jo Sonja Red.
9. Transfer details to face.
10. Paint hair, beard, mustache, eyebrows, and eyes in Soft White.
11. Add pupils to eyes in Soft Black.
12. Paint mouth in Jo Sonja Red.
13. Using Floated Color technique, paint nose and cheeks in Jo Sonja Red.

Complete the Finishing Touches

1. Glue star, moon, heart, arms, and wire assembly to Santa.
2. Apply antiquing mud. Allow to dry completely, at least 24 hours.
3. Lightly sand boots, heart, and moon to age.
4. Finish with 2 thin coats of varnish.

SANTA #3

Paint the Santa

1. Transfer general outline of pattern to ornament.
2. Paint face in Light Peaches n' Cream.
3. Paint suit and arms in Jo Sonja Red.
4. Paint heart and boots in Marina Blue.
5. Transfer details to face.
6. Paint hair, beard, mustache, eyebrows, and eyes in Soft White.
7. Add pupils to eyes in Soft Black.
8. Paint mouth in Jo Sonja Red.
9. Using Floated Color technique, paint nose and cheeks in Jo Sonja Red.
10. Paint dots on arms in Soft White.

Complete the Finishing Touches

1. Glue heart to arms and wire asembly; glue to Santa.
2. Apply antiquing mud. Allow to dry completely, at least 24 hours.
3. Lightly sand boots and heart to age.
4. Finish with 2 thin coats of varnish.

Left: Clothespin Tree Trimmers, Santas #1 and 2, Snowman #2

SANTA #2

SANTA CLOTHESPIN TREE TRIMMER
1   JO SONJA RED
2   LIGHT PEACHES N' CREAM
3   SOFT WHITE
4   MARINA BLUE
5   GOLDEN HARVEST
6   SOFT BLACK
7   PRAIRIE GREEN

191

SANTA #1

SANTA #3

৯৯৯ **Snowmen** ৯৯৯

MATERIALS

Wooden clothespin ornament kit (set of 3)
Sandpaper
Tack cloth
Sealer
Paper towels
Acrylic palette pad
Palette knife
Pencil *or* marking pen
Water containers
1″ polyfoam sponge brush
Antiquing mud (4-oz. jar) *or* Burnt Umber oil paint
Linseed oil/mineral spirits
Scrap fabric (optional)
Brushes: #1 *or* #3 round; #8 *or* #10 flat; ¼″ stencil
   brush

Graphite paper
Tracing paper
Drafting tape
Stylus
Eraser
Wood glue *or* glue gun
Twigs
Steel wool
Varnish

PALETTE

Delta Ceramcoat	*Jo Sonja Chroma*	*Illinois Bronze*
Antique White	★	Antique White
Black	Carbon Black	Soft Black
Pumpkin	★	True Orange
Burnt Sienna	Burnt Sienna	Burnt Sienna
Bright Red	Napthol Red Light	Jo Sonja Red
Straw	Yellow Oxide + White	Golden Harvest
Green Isle	Brilliant Green	Holiday Green
Colonial Blue	Aqua	Marina Blue

DIRECTIONS

To prepare for this project, please read and follow the General Instructions and Basic Procedures for all projects (beginning on page 200) and the instructions for those particular Special Techniques used in this project (beginning on page 206).

Note: Arms and wire assembly may be removed for easier painting.

SNOWMAN #1

Paint the Snowman

1. Paint snowman (except hat) in Soft White.
2. Transfer pattern or sketch on details.
3. Paint hat, eyes, mouth, buttons, and boots in Soft Black.
4. Paint nose in True Orange.
5. Using stencil brush and Dry Brush Color technique, paint cheeks in Jo Sonja Red.
6. Paint heart in Jo Sonja Red.
7. Add twinkle dots to eyes in Soft White.

Complete the Finishing Touches
1. Glue heart, nose, and hat in place.
2. Apply antiquing mud. Allow to dry completely, at least 24 hours.
3. Lightly sand hat, boots, and heart to age.
4. Glue in twig arms.
5. Finish with 2 thin coats of varnish.
6. Tie scrap fabric around neck for scarf.

Above: Clothespin Tree Trimmers, Snowmen #1 and 3, Santa #3

SNOWMAN #2

Paint the Snowman
1. Paint snowman (except hat) and arms in Soft White.
2. Transfer pattern or sketch on details.
3. Paint hat, eyes, mouth, buttons, and boots in Soft Black.
4. Paint nose in True Orange.
5. Using stencil brush and Dry Brush Color technique, paint cheeks in Jo Sonja Red.
6. Using wood end of brush, paint dots on arms in Jo Sonja Red.
7. Paint star in Golden Harvest.
8. Add twinkle dots to eyes in Soft White.

Complete the Finishing Touches
1. Glue star, hat, and nose in place.
2. Apply antiquing mud. Allow to dry completely, at least 24 hours.
3. Lightly sand star, hat, and boots to age.
4. Glue arms and wire asembly in place.
5. Finish with 2 thin coats of varnish.

SNOWMAN #3

Paint the Snowman
1. Paint snowman (except hat) in Soft White.
2. Transfer pattern or sketch on details.
3. Paint hat, eyes, mouth, buttons, and boots in Soft Black.
4. Paint nose in True Orange.
5. Using stencil brush and Dry Brush Color technique, paint cheeks in Jo Sonja Red.
6. Paint heart in Jo Sonja Red.
7. Add twinkle dots to eyes in Soft White.

Complete the Finishing Touches
1. Glue heart and nose in place.
2. Apply antiquing mud. Allow to dry completely, at least 24 hours.
3. Lightly sand hat, boots, and heart to age.
4. Glue twig arms in place.
5. Finish with 2 thin coats of varnish.
6. Tie scrap fabric around neck for scarf.

SNOWMEN CLOTHESPIN TREE TRIMMERS
1 SOFT WHITE
2 SOFT BLACK
3 GOLDEN HARVEST
4 JO SONJA RED
5 TRUE ORANGE

SNOWMAN #1

TWINKLE DOT

USE TWIGS
FOR SNOWMAN #1

SNOWMAN #3

TWIGS

USE STAR FOR SNOWMAN #2

195

Merry Tic-Tac-Toe Gameboard

My children have grown up and out of children's toys. But now my nieces and nephews need fun things to do when visiting. Tic-tac-toe is fun and children need only a short lesson and they're ready to go. The snowmen and pine trees appeal to them, and I think they also appreciate the artistic effort that went into this set.

MATERIALS

Wooden tic-tac-toe board; game pieces
Sandpaper
Tack cloth
Sealer
Paper towels
Acrylic palette pad
Palette knife
Water containers
Round toothpicks
1″ polyfoam sponge brush
Antiquing mud (4-oz. jar) *or* Burnt Umber oil paint
Linseed oil/mineral spirits
Scruffy old toothbrush *or* stencil brush
Brushes: #8 *or* #12 flat

Pencil *or* marking pen
White transfer paper
Tracing paper
Drafting tape
Stylus
Eraser
Ruler
Steel wool
Varnish

PALETTE

Delta Ceramcoat	*Jo Sonja Chroma*	*Illinois Bronze*
Woodland Night	★	Prairie Green
Bright Red	Napthol Red Light	Jo Sonja Red
Antique White	Titanium White	Antique White
Black	Carbon Black	Soft Black
Pumpkin	★	True Orange

DIRECTIONS

To prepare for this project, please read and follow the General Instructions and Basic Procedures for all projects (beginning on page 200) and the instructions for those particular Special Techniques used in this project (beginning on page 206).

Note: You may wish to add extra character to this project by using the Distressing technique to make a few gouges or scrapes in the game board and pieces.

Paint the Box and Add Lettering

1. Paint the outside of the box Antique White.
2. Transfer checkerboard pattern and inset for lettering to one side of box.
3. Using the pattern from step 2 above, omit inset for lettering and extend and transfer checkerboard lines to remaining 3 sides of board.
4. Paint frame around inset in Jo Sonja Red.
5. Add lettering in Soft Black.
6. Add dots after the words TIC and TAC in Jo Sonja Red.

197

7. Paint alternate squares on the outside of the box in Prairie Green.
8. Paint the inside edge of the box in Prairie Green.
9. Paint the top edges of the box in Jo Sonja Red.
10. Paint the squares in the four corners of the top edges of the box in Soft Black.
11. Add a dot to the center of each Soft Black square in Antique White.

Paint the Playing Board and Game Pieces
1. Paint the playing field in Jo Sonja Red.
2. Paint the trees in Prairie Green.
3. Paint the snowmen in Antique White.
4. Transfer the eyes and mouths to snowmen if needed.
5. Paint the hats, eyes, and mouths in Soft Black.

6. Paint the ends of 5 toothpicks in True Orange.
7. Sand the toothpicks lightly to age them and to dull their points.
8. Cut the toothpick ends approximately ⅜″ long.
9. Glue the toothpicks into the holes provided in the snowmen.

Complete the Finishing Touches
1. Sand the gameboard and pieces to age them.
2. Apply antiquing mud. Allow to dry completely, at least 24 hours.
3. Cover the faces of the snowmen with tiny pieces of paper towel and spatter all pieces—first in Antique White and then in Black.
4. Finish with 2 thin coats of varnish.

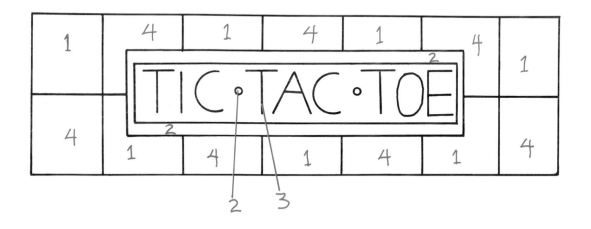

MERRY TIC-TAC-TOE GAMEBOARD
1   ANTIQUE WHITE
2   JO SONJA RED
3   SOFT BLACK
4   PRAIRIE GREEN
5   TRUE ORANGE

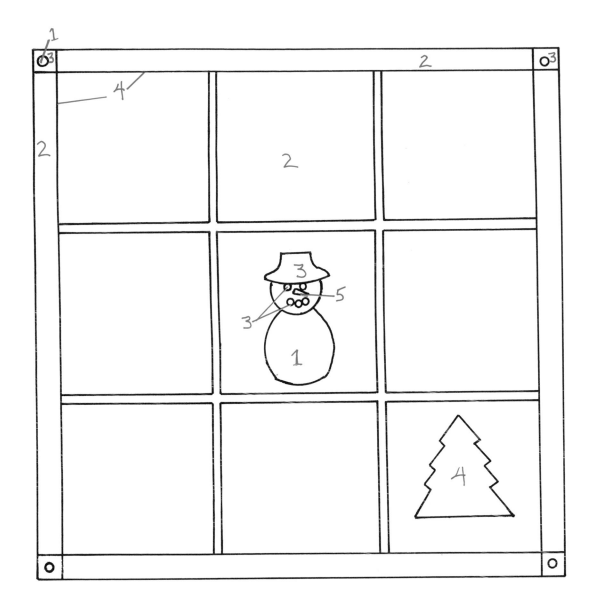

All About
Painting Country Woodcrafts

General Instructions and Basic Procedures

I sometimes like to remind my students that they can't "fail" folk art. The personalized quirks and styles that emerge from experience are, for me, what make the piece. Folk art or "country" painting is not a trained art, and I would like to emphasize that the terms and techniques described in this book are simply those that I have used and developed over the years.

One of the first and most important factors to consider when you decide you want to paint crafts is where you will do the painting. It is very desirable to create a permanent work area for yourself. Pick a spot in the kitchen, family room, bedroom, utility room, or basement, preferably with good natural light. If you can arrange to have your own special area for painting, you will find that you paint more often and keep your supplies and work more orderly.

It's also convenient to have a container large enough to carry all your supplies in case you have the occasion to paint with friends or outdoors. I use a sturdy basket with two handles that I bought at the fruit growers co-op at a reasonable price. I can add, take out, and change supplies to suit my needs.

There are some general procedures that should be considered for most, if not all, painting projects, even the simplest ones. In this section, I explain procedures to be completed before you start to paint, how to transfer a pattern onto the wooden piece, some basic terms and techniques of painting, and ways to enhance, complete, and protect the final product. Additional painting methods are discussed under Special Techniques, page 206.

Procedures
Before Painting

Before you actually begin to paint the wooden pieces, there are several steps you should take or at least consider taking. They will make the painting stages easier and more effective.

SURFACE PREPARATION AND SEALING
The surface of any wood piece should be prepared for paint. The amount of preparation needed varies,

depending on how the wood has been commercially prepared or whether you have crafted it yourself. Either way, the time spent preparing and sealing the surface is well worth it in the long run.

First, repair any blemishes you find in the wood, using medium-grit sandpaper and wood filler, if needed. Always sand *with* the grain. After blemishes have been repaired, switch to fine sandpaper and lightly sand all surfaces of the piece, paying particular attention to the edges. Remove the sanding dust with a tack cloth.

The surfaces are now ready to be sealed. Unless you are specifically instructed not to seal a piece, you should complete this preliminary step before starting to paint. Sealing is desirable for several reasons. First, it helps to keep paint from soaking into the wood, thus allowing you to use less paint. Second, it provides a smooth "canvas" for your paints.

Sealing is particularly important on soft porous woods such as pine; these woods perform best only when sealed. Sealing is essential on previously painted surfaces. They must be sanded and sealed to give new paint a surface to adhere to.

Seal wood surfaces with a sponge brush using smooth and even strokes. Be careful on the edges so that you don't form a ridge of liquid. After the sealer has dried, sand the piece lightly and then remove all dust with a tack cloth (see Source Guide, page 214).

A special note: For the sake of economy of space, not all drying steps are specified in the project's directions. However, it is imperative that you allow each layer of paint for a particular area or step to dry completely before painting or finishing on top of it, or you will end up removing it. Drying time varies with climate and thickness of paint, but can be speeded up with a blow dryer. Wait until the paint feels bone-dry to the touch before you paint over it.

BASECOATING

Basecoating refers to the coats of paint applied to a wood surface after it has been prepared for painting by sanding and sealing. The projects in this book call for 2 coats unless otherwise specified.

When basecoating, be sure to use an appropriately sized brush (usually polyfoam sponge) and apply the paint *with* the grain in even strokes, "pulling" paint across the surface. Take care to prevent ridges from forming on the edges. Allow the first basecoat to dry completely—that is, bone-dry—before applying the second coat. You can speed up drying time by using a blow dryer set on medium heat and held 8 to 12 inches from the surface. After the first coat has dried, allow it to cool down (if you have used a dryer), then sand very lightly with a piece of grocery bag or used fine-grit sandpaper. Then, remove dust with a tack cloth, apply a second basecoat, let dry, and sand lightly again. Finally, remove all sanding dust with the tack cloth.

Transferring
ཞའཞ Patterns ཞའཞ

Before beginning any project, read through the transferring and painting directions. Depending on the complexity of the painted design, you may transfer the entire pattern to the wood piece at the beginning or you may transfer different elements at different times during the painting process. I usually suggest that you transfer the general outline of the design first—say, a snowman with his hat, head, and body outlines. Paint those areas and let them dry before you transfer details such as the snowman's eyes, nose, and buttons.

Use paper clips to secure tracing paper to the page you wish to transfer. Use a fine-tip marking pen or pencil to trace the pattern lines in the book. Be careful not to shift the tracing paper or accidentally increase the pattern areas, and be especially accurate with facial features.

Position the tracing paper carefully onto the wooden piece and secure it with drafting tape on two sides. Then, slip graphite paper or white transfer paper between the wood piece and the tracing paper and secure both ends with tape. Use a small stylus to draw over the traced pattern exactly as you did before, taking care not to mar the wood.

Basic Painting
Procedures

Before opening a container of paint, shake it very well. Squeeze out a small amount onto the palette. This "puddle" will be your working supply of paint. Choose the type and size of brush needed for the part you are going to paint and work the brush back and forth in the puddle. This step is called **loading** or **dressing** the brush. There are several special ways of loading a brush to achieve particular effects. These methods, such as double-loaded and side-loaded, are discussed under Special Techniques, page 206.

Paint should generally be applied with smooth, even strokes, following the grain of the wood or the contours of the piece. Special types of strokes can be used to achieve particular effects. One special stroke used in some projects in this book is what I call the **comma stroke**, such as those used on the Victorian Heart Jewelry Box lid (page 120). To make a comma stroke, use a #3 or #5 round brush, load the brush with paint, and rotate it against the palette to distribute the paint throughout the bristles and return the bristles to their original shape. Start at the fattest part of the design element you wish to color and pull the brush toward you with a slight curve, lifting it up slightly as you taper off of the surface to complete the stroke. A **petal stroke** may be achieved in the same manner by pulling the stroke straight toward you, without curving it.

Linework and dot designs are used in many projects. To do **linework**, first thin paint to the consistency of light cream. When you have obtained the consistency you want, rotate the bristles into their original shape and paint faint, long, curvy lines on practice paper. The amount of pressure you use will determine the thickness of the line. When you are satisfied with the result, proceed to the linework on the piece.

A **dot design** can be made with the wood end of a brush, the bristle end of a round brush, or a stylus. The size of the dotting tool determines the size of the dots. For a dot design, thin the paint to the consistency of light cream and practice dabbing the paint until it neither "peaks" like beaten egg whites nor bleeds because it is too thin.

MIXING PAINTS

Mixing 2 or more different paints allows you to create additional colors. When preparing to mix paints, be sure to shake the containers of paint before squeezing any paint out onto the palette. The mix "recipes" given in the project instructions give specific amounts, called **parts**, for each color. A part is a measurement equal to the size of an M & M candy. However, adjustments may be necessary to obtain the exact

Comma Stroke

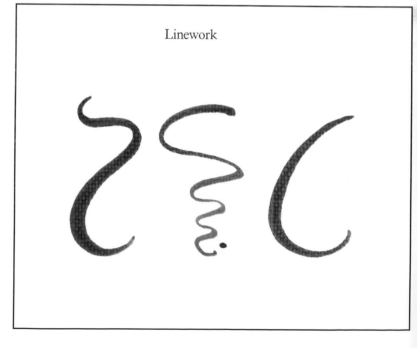

Linework

202

color you wish. A pink mixture may, for example, be lightened by adding white, darkened by adding red, or subdued by adding a dab of blue or green. Refer to the color photos of the pieces when mixing paints—or make adjustments based on your color preferences. In some cases, a mix gives best results if the paints are not completely mixed; the project directions will specify this. Repeat to mix additional paint as needed. Cover mixes with plastic wrap between applications.

THINNING PAINT

In some applications, such as linework and dot designs, paint must be thinned. There is no definite recipe for thinning paint. You have to experiment until you achieve the desired consistency—usually of light cream. Begin by dispensing 1 part paint onto the palette. Dip the wood end of a #1 or #2 liner into water and let 1 drop of water drip into the paint. Mix lightly with a palette knife and repeat as necessary to achieve the desired consistency. Use a practice paper and faint, long, curvy lines. When you are satisfied with the consistency of the paint and the result, proceed to the project.

SPONGE PAINTING

The sponging technique is used in several projects. Wet the sponge in clear water and squeeze out as much of the water as you can by blotting the sponge on paper towels. The sponge should be damp, not wet. Hold the sponge between your thumb, first, and second fingers, and dip it into a fresh puddle of paint. Blot the sponge lightly on paper towels to remove excess paint and lightly pat the sponge onto the work. (It is best to practice on paper before going to the piece to be painted.) Use a soft touch and work quickly. Turn the sponge with every application for freedom of design. You will probably need to reload the sponge every 3 to 6 pats. Repeat the entire procedure until the piece is completely painted.

If you should get a blob of color from too heavy an application, simply allow it to dry. While it is drying, clean the sponge, blot until towel damp, dip into the basecoat color, and apply to cover the blob. Then, let that dry and continue the sponging procedure as before.

STAINING

Commercial stains are readily available in a wide range of colors. However, you can make your own by mixing Burnt Umber oil paint, Burnt Sienna oil paint, or any color you choose with mineral spirits and a small amount of linseed oil in a small container. Apply stain with a soft brush or cloth and wipe off excess.

SHADING

In this book, the areas to be shaded are indicated on the pattern by small dots clustered together. The Floated Color technique (see page 207) is often used for shading. Follow the specific directions for each project.

Procedures
After Painting

Wait until the painted surfaces are bone-dry. Remove any visible chalk or graphite lines with a cotton swab dipped in mineral spirits. **Do not** use an eraser to remove lines, as it will leave a residue and mar your finish. Then, proceed with distressing, aging, antiquing, varnishing, and any other special finishing procedures.

DISTRESSING

Distressing gives a piece a used, old, antique-ish look. It can actually be done at any point—before preparing to paint, before basecoats, or just before antiquing. I occasionally distress a piece just before antiquing because I'll discover after painting that it needs a little something extra.

Distressing can be done with several types of tools. I've used a screwdriver tip and coins to gouge, a screwdriver handle to make dents, keys to make scratches and dents, and a small hammer to assault edges. I have learned from experience to always gouge *with* the grain of the wood to avoid injury. If you distress after painting and before antiquing, sand the distress markings to remove burrs.

SANDING TO AGE

A piece can be aged by lightly sanding after painting. In fact, the instructions frequently recommend sanding edges and other areas of a piece that would develop worn spots over time before going on to the antiquing process. Sometimes sanding will remove several layers of paint to expose raw wood. Never sand the entire outside edge of a piece or develop a ring of raw white wood: Nothing except a wheel gets so uniformly worn. The sanded areas will usually be subdued with antiquing.

ANTIQUING

Most of the pieces described in this book are antiqued. This technique gently ages a piece and makes it appear softer and more refined. Antiquing also enhances color, adds character, and creates depth and highlights, especially in nicks, grooves, and crannies. Antiquing is much more than simply darkening a piece with "mud."

In this book, antiquing is usually completed before varnishing. Commercial antiquing media are widely available in craft/hobby stores. The product I prefer is a linseed oil–based solution called Mud. I prefer the darkest of the three shades available. You can substitute Burnt Umber oil paint mixed with linseed oil or mineral spirits for commercial antiquing mud, if you prefer.

Other supplies needed for antiquing are an appropriately sized bristle or sponge brush, clean rags or soft paper towels, cotton swabs, and a coffee can with a lid to house used rags. Do not allow used rags to remain unprotected or leave them in a trash bag. A protective apron and rubber gloves are also needed. If you use a bristle brush, be sure to clean it in mineral spirits immediately after use.

Always antique in a well-ventilated area. Dip a clean rag into the solution, and apply it following the manufacturer's directions. Whether you apply it liberally or sparingly, cover an entire area at one time, to avoid overlap and unevenness. For example, if you are antiquing a box, treat the entire top at one time, then move to a side, and so forth. You can use straight or circular strokes—I've never noticed any difference. Using the cloth, blend the antiquing mud evenly across the area to achieve an opaque look. Wait a few seconds and then start removing the antiquing with a clean cloth, constantly moving toward new areas. A clean cloth will prevent you from redepositing mud onto an area you have just wiped.

Remove as much or as little of the mud as you prefer—from a small section of the piece or from the entire piece. Allow the mud to remain heaviest or darkest in

Supplies for Antiquing

areas that you feel should be enhanced and wherever natural shade would be expected to occur, such as under a collar, under an apron, and between a sleeve and shirt. Nooks and crannies are also good places for heavier layers of mud. Remove almost all antiquing from any areas that have been aged with sandpaper.

If you have difficulty in removing mud from an area that you wish to appear lighter, slightly dampen a cotton swab or a corner of a rag with linseed oil or mineral spirits. Blot the swab or rag and wipe over the area. I prefer the afterglow and tonal appeal that linseed oil imparts to the work, and its longer drying time makes it easier to control than mineral spirits.

As a final step, use a mop brush to lightly skim the surface of the work, smoothing and blending away any impressions left from your cloth, and softening the antiquing to give the piece a uniform look. Drying time for the antiquing process can take from 24 hours to 7 days or longer, depending on the depth of antiquing and the climate in your region. I recommend waiting as long as possible before varnishing, to be safest.

Some projects call for the antiquing to be finished by highlighting to emphasize some of the features of the piece. Various highlighting techniques are explained under Special Techniques, page 206 .

DETAILING
Fine detailing refers to the last bit of embellishing done with paint and a brush or with a pen. These touches often replace small details that may have been removed in the antiquing process. Some examples are twinkle dots added to an eye, or areas of brighter color added to lips or leaves. This type of detailing is usually done freehand.

VARNISHING
Varnish gives all painted objects a finished look and helps to protect them. Spray varnish in a matte or satin finish is my preference, but you may want a different type. Buy the best quality you can afford—you want your work to be well protected.

When all painted areas have been decorated, dried, and allowed to rest for 24 hours (1 week for pieces that are antiqued), you can begin to varnish. Cover the work area with newspapers and place your piece on a grocery bag. Make sure you have adequate ventilation. Then, following the manufacturer's directions, spray on a light coat of varnish. Let the varnish dry.

2 or 3 coats of varnish is normal for a piece that will be handled a lot, and 3 to 5 coats is not unusual for outdoor pieces. After the first coat of varnish has dried, rub extra-fine steel wool (size #0000) very lightly across the surface. Then, wipe with a tack cloth to remove dust and apply a second light coat of varnish. You may wish to rub with steel wool a second time. Wear rubber gloves to keep the steel wool dust off your hands.

WAXING
Wait one or two weeks after varnishing before applying paste wax. A coat of good paste wax not only adds a nice sheen to the painted piece but also protects the work and enhances the colors. Pieces that are to be exposed to the weather should always be waxed to extend their lives. Apply the wax 2–3 weeks before placing the piece outdoors, and renew once a year.

EMBELLISHING
In this book, embellishing refers to extra items on a finished painted piece. The embellishments may be wood or other scrap material, such as a scarf, or twig arms for a snowman. Remember to keep the colors of the embellishments in harmony with those of the paint palette.

Before gluing on an embellishment, sand the surfaces to be joined; glue will not adhere to varnish.

A reminder: Be sure you take time to read all of the General Instructions and Basic Procedures, along with the section on Basic Equipment, before beginning a project, as important steps and directions required for a successful outcome are discussed in these sections. Read the Materials list to be sure you have all the items needed and the Directions to be sure you understand them.

Special Techniques

There are many methods of loading paint, painting special strokes, and producing different effects that add special character to specific pieces. The techniques used in the projects in this book are described below. Before applying any of these techniques, be certain that the piece is bone-dry.

OUTLINE-AND-PAINT TECHNIQUE

Often applied after antiquing, this highlighting technique is used to clean up, define, or make a detail more noticeable. This can often mean applying a brighter color to the outlines of a specific design element such as hair or leaves; sometimes the original color of the element may be used. In either case, the color will be specified in the project Directions. For example, the Autumn Sunflower Crate (page 67) uses a #3 round brush to apply True Orange to one side of some of the sunflower petals, thus adding more interest and fullness to the petals. This is repeated randomly so that you create interest and not a picket fence effect. Some of the linework and leaves in the Victorian Heart Wastebasket project (page 129), are highlighted by outlining. In all outline-and-paint highlighting, remember to apply color randomly, and that "less is more."

This technique is also used to repaint narrow linework and details (a cheek for example) that may have been rubbed off during the antiquing process. To begin this process after antiquing, you must prepare a fresh surface for the highlight paint to adhere to, by very lightly "sanding" the specific area to be highlighted, that is, removing any antiquing using a piece of paper towel or brown paper bag. For very fine lines a very worn emery board may be used. Then, use paint and a brush to apply strokes to the area.

STENCIL BRUSH HIGHLIGHTING OR DRY BRUSH COLOR TECHNIQUE

I use this technique and an appropriately sized stencil brush to add soft color to a specific spot—a cheek, for

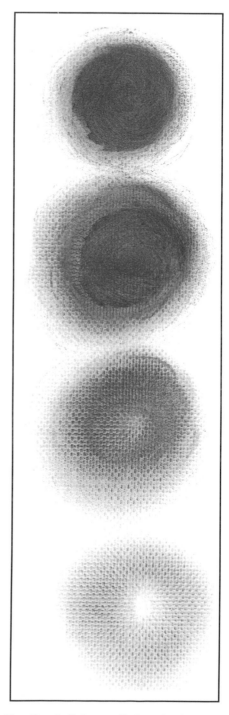

Dry Brush Color applied to cheeks with stencil brush

206

example. Dampen the brush, press out as much water as possible, and blot well. Hold the brush perpendicular to the paint puddle, dip brush into paint and, on practice paper, use a circular motion to distribute paint throughout the bristles, first clockwise then counterclockwise, continually moving to an unpainted area. When only a very small amount of paint remains on the bristles, apply to piece, using a circular motion or a patting/tapping motion, whichever you find more comfortable. Repeat the entire procedure for greater depth of color, as desired.

Stencil highlighting can also be used to add extra interest after antiquing. To highlight a red apple, for example, simply dip the stencil brush in True Orange and apply the paint to one side of the apple. Still more interest can be added by stencil-brushing Bordeaux on the other side of the apple, thus creating an interesting shaded "depth" to an object, as in the Apple-Lemon Heart Clock (page 93).

SPATTERING
In this book, the term spattering (sometimes called fly specking) refers to the application of fine, irregular dots to a particular area of a piece or to an entire piece. Spattering is used to add color and texture, to subdue color, to give a piece unity, and/or to age a piece. Areas that you do not wish to spatter—faces and flowers, for example—should be covered with appropriately sized pieces of paper towel.

Spattering can be done with just 1 color or with as many as 4 or 5 colors. When using more than 1 color, start with the lightest and work from light to dark. Spattering is best done with a stiff ½"–¾" stencil brush or an old scruffy toothbrush. Always use colors from the project palette.

Dampen the brush with water, blot well, dip it into the paint, and run a pencil or your thumbnail over the bristles while directing them toward the surface you wish to spatter. Hold the brush about 8 to 10 inches above the work. The farther away from the piece you hold the brush, the finer the spatters will be. Check for droplets emerging from the brush or pencil. If any hit your work or a glob of unwanted paint is accidentally deposited on the work, wipe it off immediately with a damp towel or cotton swab. You can add as much spattering as you like, but remember, spattering is generally more appealing if less, rather than more, is applied. **A word of caution:** Practice spattering on newspaper until you feel confident about the size and pattern of specks you want to place on the actual piece.

FLOATED COLOR TECHNIQUE
This technique is used most often for shading and occasionally for highlighting. Wet a flat brush (#8, #10, or #12 is best) in clear water and then very gently blot the chisel edge of the bristles on paper towel, allowing a water sheen to remain on the bristles but not on the ferrule (this will cause paint to bleed). Dip one corner of the brush into the paint and blend several times in the same spot on a damp palette using care not to lose too much paint. Apply to the surface with the paint side of the brush on edge of the motif you wish to shade. The paint will blend from color to water (clear), or in other words, will float out. Clean the brush and repeat the procedure for each stroke.

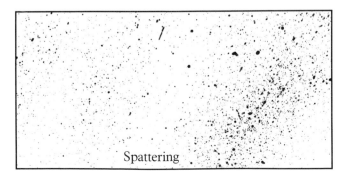

Spattering

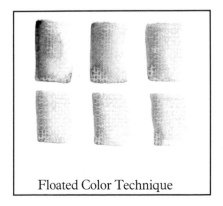

Floated Color Technique

DOUBLE-LOADED COLOR TECHNIQUE

This technique allows you to apply two paints at the same time. I use it primarily for flowers and leaves. Load a flat brush in one color and then dip the corner of the brush into the second color. Blend with 2 strokes on the palette pad and apply to piece. Wipe brush with a towel and repeat as needed. For **Triple-Loaded Color Technique**, dip opposite corner of brush in the third color before blending.

Double-Loaded Color Technique

SIDE-LOADED COLOR TECHNIQUE

In this technique, sometimes used in highlighting, the paint is simply loaded onto only one side of a flat brush. Highlighting added to one side of a cheek (see St. Nick's Christmas Card Holder, page 178) is an example of where to apply this technique.

CROSS-HATCHING

To make a crosshatch pattern, load a flat brush with paint and remove most of the paint by stroking on practice paper. Then apply the brush to the area to be cross-hatched in a north-south direction. Reload and repeat if the first application is too faint. Reload, stroke on practice paper, and then apply paint in an east-west direction.

TRANSPARENT WASH

This technique allows you to apply a very thin coat of subtle color to a piece. Dispense 1 part desired color of paint onto your palette. Create a puddle of clear water (about 5 tablespoons) nearby on the palette. Dip one small corner of a glaze brush size ¾"–1½" (I prefer Robert Simmons brand) into the paint; mix with water. The paint will immediately begin to spread through the water. Saturate the brush with the diluted paint, then apply to the piece with smooth, wide strokes. Repeat until you have acquired the intensity and variation of color you prefer. Don't worry if the application is a little uneven—this adds character to the piece.

Paints, Brushes, and Other Equipment

Paints

The projects in this book use acrylic paints that are well suited for wooden surfaces. Acrylic paint is water-based, which allows simple thinning with water, easy cleanup, and a fast drying time. Although acrylic paints dry faster than oil-based paints, they don't dry so quickly that you can't work with them in a relaxed manner. If you find you need additional working time, incorporate a drop or two of retarder into the puddle of paint on your palette. (I rarely use retarder, but I keep it handy just in case.)

The colors you use on a particular piece strongly influence the personality and character of that piece and will, in most cases, reflect your personality and lifestyle. If, however, you are painting a piece for someone other than yourself, try to think of that piece in relation to that person and select colors accordingly. The only constant I've found is that children are universally fond of purple and pink!

The general palettes manufactured today provide a complete and extensive, if somewhat confusing, array of colors. For this reason, a color group of paints is given for each project. In time and with practice, you will develop your own personal palette to reflect your taste.

The brands and types of paints listed for each project—Accent Acrylics by Illinois Bronze, Jo Sonja Chroma Acrylics, and Delta Ceramcoat—are all good quality and competitively priced, so I don't recommend one over the other. Although some teachers would disagree, I have never had a problem mixing different brands, and in fact, some of the projects in this book have paints of all three brands. All three are readily available in craft shops in 2-ounce containers. Some colors are also available in larger, more economical sizes that you may want to buy in the colors you use most often. For each project, a 2-ounce container of each color listed should be ample.

A few helpful hints about paints:
- Don't let paint freeze. If it does freeze, discard it.
- Shake containers of paint thoroughly before dispensing the paint onto the palette. Be sure to keep the container lids and flap caps secure when shaking, or you'll have a mess on your clothes, the walls, and the floor.
- Wash up any spills immediately with cool water.
- Always keep paint away from children unless you are there to supervise them.

Brushes

Brushes are your most important tool, and a successful finished product depends on good tool performance. Buy the best brushes you can afford. If you care for them properly, they will last a long time.

You'll need quality synthetic bristle brushes designed for acrylic paints and water. I like Robert Simmons and Loew Cornell brands. These brushes come with sizing in them, which should be rinsed out before they are used.

CHOOSING AN ASSORTMENT
To begin a brush collection and to complete the projects in this book, an assortment of each of the following types of brushes is recommended:

Polyfoam sponges
Polyfoam sponge brushes are used to apply paint to boxes, signs, or any surface larger than an ornament or magnet. Use long, even strokes and watch the edges

for drips and runs. Dampen the brush in clear water, expel excess water, blot, dip into the paint, and apply paint to the piece *with* the grain of the wood. Usually, 2 coats per surface area are needed. Polyfoam sponge brushes don't last long, but they are inexpensive. Buy several 1″–1½″ wide.

Flats

Flat brushes are very versatile with endless applications. The distinctive chiselled edge is used to paint areas such as faces, roses, leaves, gowns, trees, and checkerboards. Flats are also used to apply Floated Color shading. Use a size appropriate to the area to be covered. Begin by purchasing sizes #8 and #10. Later, you may want to add sizes #4, #6, and #12.

Rounds

Round brushes are used to paint hair, florals, eyebrows, eyelashes, veins in leaves, and lip and nose outlines. They are also perfect for comma strokes. Use the size appropriate to the area to be covered. Start by purchasing sizes #1, #3, and #5.

Liners

Liner brushes are used for linework, outlining, and scrolling. The width of the line is determined by the width of the bristles. Use the size appropriate to the line to be painted. Begin by purchasing size #1.

Mops

Mops are used to lightly brush across the surface of a just-antiqued piece. Brush in a circular motion to eliminate starkness and to homogenize and enrich the piece. Clean the brush in mineral spirits immediately after use.

Stencil brushes

Stencil brushes are used in this book to apply highlights, primarily cheek and nose color. Use a size appropriate to the area to be highlighted, as specified in the Materials lists. Begin with ¼″, ⅜″ or ⅝″, and ¾″ brushes.

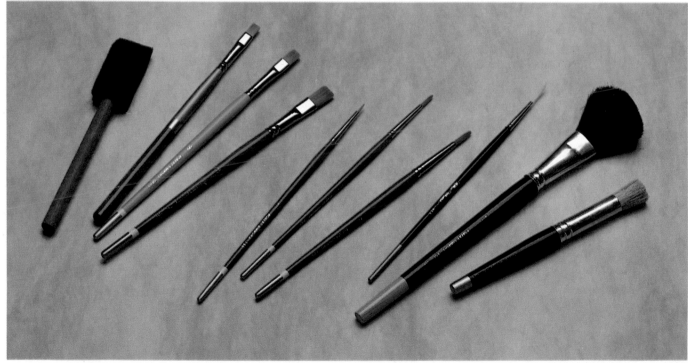

Brushes, *left to right:* Polyfoam sponge, flats, rounds, liner, mop and stencil

CARING FOR BRUSHES

Brushes should be kept clean and in their original shape. Always clean brushes immediately after use, as acrylic paint dries very fast and quickly hardens on brushes. After you have finished painting for the day, wash brushes out with clear cool water and bar soap or a commercial paint remover (see Source Guide, page 214). Work up a good lather and press bristles against the palm of your hand until all traces of color are gone. Be very gentle—don't bend bristles or push too hard. Always coax the brush into its original shape and store it in a special brush keeper (see "Miscellaneous Equipment," below). When cleaning or rinsing a brush, always use cool water. Hot water will set paint into the bristles and eventually loosen them.

Flush brushes out frequently during a painting session, and always try to keep paint away from the ferrule, the point where the bristles meet the metal. If you do get paint near the ferrule, clean it off immediately.

You should never allow paint to harden on a brush, but if it does happen, dip the brush into rubbing alcohol and wipe on a paper towel. Repeat the process until the bristles are clean. Then, shape the bristles and return the brush to the brush holder. Alcohol is hard on brushes, so make every effort to avoid this method of cleaning.

While you are painting, brushes not actually in use should be kept in water at all times. I highly recommend using a brush basin. This water-filled device allows you to rest brushes in water without bending the bristles and is helpful to remove fresh paint. If you are interrupted during a painting session and have no time to flush the paint out of your brush, you can place the brush in the basin and the paint will be kept from hardening. Never stand your brush in a jar of water: The bristles will bend and conform to the contour of the bottom of the jar.

Miscellaneous
༄ Equipment ༄

In addition to the basics—a wooden piece, paint, and brushes—several other tools and pieces of equipment that are needed to complete projects in this book. Most are available in crafts supply stores or hardware stores; some are simple household items that you probably already have. Although I have attempted to make this list complete, you may sometimes need some additional items. Refer to this basic list and to the Materials list at the beginning of each project before starting to work. Be sure you have everything you might need easily accessible. Nothing is quite so annoying as being in the middle of a painting project and finding that you must stop and search for or buy some item you need.

Water containers

At least 2 glass or plastic water containers, each able to hold 10 to 12 ounces, are needed for any painting project. One container is needed for cleaning brushes when changing colors and a second is for clear water, which you will use to thin paint, to wet brushes, and for the Floated Color technique (see page 207).

Acrylic palette pad

A pad on which to dispense dollops of paint is essential. A palette pad can be purchased at crafts supply shops or art supply stores. Keep the palette covered between painting sessions.

Spritzer bottle

A bottle that can hold at least 6 ounces of water and sprays a fine mist is best. You can purchase it in a crafts or beauty supply store. Use it to mist paints on the palette pad to help them stay moist and prevent their drying out. Misting and then covering the pad with a thoroughly moistened paper towel will keep paints moist for about half an hour.

Plastic container with lid

A container large enough to house the palette pad and paint is convenient for temporary storage. Before closing the lid, cover the paints with a thoroughly moistened paper towel. This method keeps paints moist for about one or two days (length of time will vary with climate).

Palette knife

This very handy tool with a flexible metal blade is used to mix colors and to incorporate water into paints.

Transparent tracing paper

Most of the projects require a pattern to be transferred to the wood piece. Place transparent tracing paper over the pattern provided in the book and trace the design exactly as shown. Then, tape it to the wood piece.

White transfer paper

This paper helps transfer the traced pattern to the surface of darker wood pieces. Place it chalk side down underneath the tracing paper and retrace the pattern. (If necessary, you can make your own transfer pattern by rubbing the back side of the traced pattern with chalk.) Transfer paper can be reused for several projects.

Graphite paper

This paper functions like white transfer paper, except it is used to transfer patterns to lighter colored surfaces. Place it graphite side down under the tracing paper and retrace the pattern. (If the graphite paper is new, remove any excess dust by wiping gently with a tissue.) This paper can be reused for several projects.

Drafting tape

Because it is easily removed, drafting tape, or mending tape, works well to secure traced patterns to wood pieces.

Pencil or marking pen

A pencil or fine-tipped black marking pen is needed to trace the patterns onto tracing paper.

Double-ended stylus

This convenient tool is used to retrace traced patterns onto the wood surface and also to paint dots for eyes, a dotted pattern, etc.

Paper towels

Always a good idea to keep handy, paper towels are useful for wiping up spills, blotting extra paint, removing antiquing, and countless other things.

Retarder

Retarder is a clear medium that keeps acrylic paints moist, allowing you to paint as slowly as you wish. Even if you seldom use it, it's worth having on hand.

Linseed oil and/or mineral spirits

These products are used to highlight a piece after the antiquing process. They will lift antiquing mud from an area or areas you wish to highlight. Linseed oil is always used sparingly; a teaspoon is enough for a very large piece. Dip a cotton swab or rag in the linseed oil and blot several times to remove excess oil before application.

I prefer linseed oil to mineral spirits because it has a richer, mellower, and warmer finishing effect. However, mineral spirits will speed up the drying process and impart a sharper, more primitive, unrefined look, which is currently preferred by many people. Mineral spirits also function as an effective cleaner for oil- or petroleum distillate–based products. Many people these days use odorless turpentine as a substitute for mineral spirits. If you choose this medium, use extra caution as it is easily mistaken for water.

Antiquing mud

Commercial antiquing mud is used in many projects to create an old "used" look. Burnt Umber oil paint may be substituted in many cases for commercial antiquing mud.

Soft clean rags

Old dishcloths, diapers, and T-shirts make good rags for applying and removing antiquing. Cut the rags into convenient 4-inch squares. A strong word of caution: Antiquing products are extremely combustible. Always dispose of rags properly. **Do not** simply throw them away in a trash can. I store my used rags in tightly covered coffee cans and bring them to an oil-recycling station for proper disposal.

Spray varnish

Varnish gives all painted objects a finished look. Matte or satin finish is my preference, but other types such as glossy finishes are available.

Sandpaper

As sandpaper is needed for surface preparation and sometimes for other steps in the painting and decorating process, I advise buying two different grains. Fine-grit sandpaper will suffice for preparing most purchased wood pieces, but you will probably need medium grit for sanding projects that you make yourself. Sandpaper is also used to "age" a project.

Sanding block

This convenient device makes sanding much easier, by providing a solid object around which you can wrap and grip the sandpaper.

Steel wool

Available at hardware stores, steel wool (size #0000) is essential for a smooth finish and provides a piece with a special patina. Lightly rub the piece between the first and second coats of varnish and again after the last coat. Be sure that each coat of finish is bone-dry before rubbing, and wear rubber gloves to prevent steel slivers from irritating your skin.

Tack cloth

This sticky oil-saturated cloth is used to remove dust from freshly sanded pieces. Cover a tack cloth with plastic wrap when not in use to prevent it from drying out prematurely.

Wood filler

Wood filler repairs small blemishes in wood. It is applied before the first sanding during the surface preparation phase.

Brown bag

Good for very light sanding, a simple brown grocery bag is effective on painted areas or between basecoats. Tear unprinted areas of a brown grocery bag into manageable pieces. Discard when fibers begin to show.

Water-based sealer

Apply a water-based sealer before painting. It keeps paint from soaking into raw wood and prepares previously painted surfaces for new color.

Paste wax

Paste wax protects wood pieces displayed outdoors from the effects of damp weather. Apply at least 2 coats of paste wax over the varnish, and rub in a fresh coat every season. Year-round indoor pieces, or any piece that seems to be losing its luster, can also be greatly enhanced with a coat of paste wax.

Rubbing alcohol

The last resort for cleaning paint brushes, rubbing alcohol can remove dried and hardened paint from brush bristles.

Brush holder

A special brush keeper or brush holder is not only convenient but also beneficial for brushes, helping them to retain their original shape. Commercial holders are available in craft stores, but you can also make your own, using a tall can (such as a potato chip can) with holes punched in the lid. Store all brushes with bristle end up; otherwise, the bristles will take on the shape of the bottom of the container.

Brush basin

This water-filled tray allows you to rest brushes horizontally while a project is in progress and keeps the paint from drying on the bristles.

Paper scissors

Scissors are used to cut patterns to fit the wood piece. (Be sure to leave a margin around the pattern so you can tape it to the piece.)

Other items

These can include a ruler, eraser, wood glue or glue gun, cotton swabs, scruffy old toothbrush, natural sea sponge, fabric scraps or ribbon, spray adhesive, thread, stapler, screwdriver, and pliers.

❧❧❧ Wood Crafts ❧❧❧

The wood crafts shown in this book are widely available in or through many crafts supply shops and from the suppliers listed in the Source Guide, page 214. You can also make many of the pieces yourself. Great satisfaction can come from making a special piece and then painting and decorating it. Then, it is truly a personal creation.

Source Guide

Paints

Illinois Bronze/Accent
Products Division
Country Colors
HPPG
Borden Inc.
Lake Zurich, IL 60047
(708) 540-1615

Delta/Ceramcoat
Delta Products
(800) 423-4135
(for a retail store
nearest you)

Jo Sonja's Artist Colors
Chroma Acrylics
205 Bucky Drive
Airport Industrial Road
Lititz, PA 17543
(717) 626-8866
Outside PA:
(800) 257-8278

Antiquing Mud

Liberty Stain and Varnish
26777 Lorain Road, #613
North Olmsted, OH 44070
(216) 779-5262

Olde Turnpike Tolehouse
No. 20
Newark Pompton Turnpike
Wayne, NJ 07470
(201) 628-1838

Varnish

Krylon Matte Finish
31500 Solon Road
Solon, OH 44139
(800) 247-3268

Varnish (matte finish)

Liberty Stain and Varnish
(see "Antiquing Mud")

Varnish (spray-on)

Illinois Bronze (see "Paints")

Sealer (all purpose)

Jo Sonja (see "Paints")

Sealer (water-based sanding sealer)

Liberty Stain and Varnish (see "Antiquing Mud")

Brushes (paint and stencil)

Roberts Simmons Inc.
45 West 18th Street
New York, NY 10011
(800) 221-9374

Combing tool

Illinois Bronze
(see "Paints")

Wood products/kits (catalogs available)

Precision Wood Products
P.O. Box 96
Elkton, OH 44415

The Wooden Hen
7389 State Route 45
Lisbon, OH 44432
(216) 424-0088

Index

All of us at Meredith® Press welcome your comments and suggestions
so that we may continue to bring you the best crafts products possible.
Please address your correspondence to:
Customer Service Department, Meredith Press, 150 East 52nd Street, New York, NY 10022
or call 1-800-678-2665.